THE WEAPONS ENCYCLOPÆDIA
TANK AIRCRAFT AFV SHIP ARTILLERY VEHICLES SECRET WEAPON

TWE-040 ENG

BATTLESHIP ROMA WWII

THE WEAPONS ENCYCLOPAEDIA

EDITORIAL STAFF
Luca Cristini, Paolo Crippa.

ACADEMIC STAFF
Enrico Acerbi, Massimiliano Afiero, Aldo Antonicelli, Ruggero Calò, Luigi Carretta, Flavio Chistè, Anna Cristini, Carlo Cucut, Matteo D'Aniello, Salvo Fagone, Enrico Finazzer, Arturo Giusti, Björn Huber, Andrea Lombardi, Aymeric Lopez, Marco Lucchetti, Maurizio Maggi, Gabriele Malavoglia, Luigi Manes, Giovanni Maressi, Francesco Mattesini, Daniele Notaro, Péter Mujzer, Federico Peirani, Alberto Peruffo, Andrea Alberto Tallillo, Antonio Tallillo, Roberto Vela, Massimo Zorza.

PUBLISHED BY
Luca Cristini Editore (Soldiershop), via Orio, 35/4 - 24050 Zanica (BG) ITALY.

DISTRIBUTION BY
Soldiershop - www.soldiershop.com, Amazon, Ingram Spark, Berliner Zinnfigurem (D), LaFeltrinelli, Mondadori, Libera Editorial (Spain), Google book (eBook), Kobo, (eBoook), Apple Book (eBook).

PUBLISHING'S NOTES
None of unpublished images or text of our book may be reproduced in any format without the expressed written permission of Luca Cristini Editore (already Soldiershop.com) when not indicate as marked with license creative commons 3.0 or 4.0. Luca Cristini Editore has made every reasonable effort to locate, contact and acknowledge rights holders and to correctly apply terms and conditions to Content. Every effort has been made to trace the copyright of all the photographs. If there are unintentional omissions, please contact the publisher in writing at: info@soldiershop.com, who will correct all subsequent editions.

LICENSES COMMONS
This book may utilize part of material marked with license creative commons 3.0 or 4.0 (CC BY 4.0), (CC BY-ND 4.0), (CC BY-SA 4.0) or (CC0 1.0). We give appropriate attribution credit and indicate if change were made in the acknowledgments field. Our WTW books series utilize only fonts licensed under the SIL Open Font License or other free use license.

CONTRIBUTORS OF THIS VOLUME & ACKNOWLEDGEMENTS
We would like to thank the main contributors to this edition: the ship profiles are all by the author. The colouring of the photos is by the author. Special thanks to national and/or private institutions such as: Army General Staff, the Italian Navy, State Archives, Bundesarchiv, Nara, Library of Congress, Wikipedia, USAF, Signal magazine, Cronache di guerra, Fronte di guerra, IWM, Australian War Museum, etc. A P.Crippa, A.Lopez, Péter Mujzer, L.Manes, C.Cucut, Tallillo archives. Model Victoria (www.modelvictoria.it) Italeri, etc. for making available pictures or anything else from their archives. Special thanks to all modellers, their clubs and modelling companies for the courtesy use of their images. As far as possible we will always include the names of the authors. Please let us know in case you have not been able to locate them.

For a complete list of Soldiershop titles, or for every information please contact us on our website: www.soldiershop.com or www.cristinieditore.com. E-mail: info@soldiershop.com. Keep up to date on Facebook https://www.facebook.com/soldiershop.publishing

Dedico questo volume alla memoria di mio zio Cristini Ernesto (detto Basilio), marinaio della regia marina durante la II'a Guerra Mondiale, catturato in operazione dagli inglesi. prigioniero in Egitto, Palestina e poi Australia.   Luca Cristini Giugno 2025

A mio figlio Giovanni, sii sempre curioso arricchisci il tuo sapere ogni giorno e coltiva con amore e dedizione le tue passioni, spero di essere stato e di continuare ad essere un buon esempio per te piccolo mio. Matteo d'Aniello

Title: **Battleship Roma** Code.: **TWE-040 EN**
Series by L. S. Cristini
ISBN code: 9791255892465. First edition June 2025
THE WEAPONS ENCYCLOPAEDIA (SOLDIERSHOP) is a trademark of Luca Cristini Editore

THE WEAPONS ENCYCLOPÆDIA
TANK AIRCRAFT AFV SHIP ARTILLERY VEHICLES SECRET WEAPON

BATTLESHIP ROMA

AND OTHER BATTLESHIPS OF THE LITTORIO CLASS

LUCA STEFANO CRISTINI

BOOK SERIES FOR MODELERS & COLLECTORS

CONTENTS

Introduction .... pag. 5

The R.N. *Roma* and the Littorio class .... pag. 9

  - Umberto Pugliese and his system .... pag. 26

  - Carlo Bergamini, the admiral .... pag. 30

The end of a great ship .... pag. 35

The aircraft of the battleship *Roma* .... pag. 43

  - IMAM Ro. 43 .... pag. 45

  - Reggiane Re. 2000 .... pag. 47

The other Littorio-class ships .... pag. 51

  - *Vittorio Veneto* .... pag. 51

  - *Littorio* .... pag. 53

  - R.N. *Impero* .... pag. 56

The battleship *Roma*: the models .... pag. 59

The *Roma* in 3D .... pag. 67

Bibliography .... pag. 70

▲ The R.N. battleship *Roma*, in 1942 model camouflage livery seen from the stern side, with the crane-catapult for aircraft clearly visible, probably in the port of La Spezia.

INTRODUCTION

■ THE BATTLESHIP ROMA: PRIDE AND TRAGEDY OF THE ROYAL ITALIAN NAVY

A giant of the seas born amid wartime tensions

In the fiery geopolitical scenario that preceded World War II, Italy launched the battleship *Roma*, the third unit of the prestigious *Littorio* class. The last jewel of the Italian fleet, completed in June 1942, this behemoth of the deep, however, never had the opportunity to prove its worth in battle. Her cruel fate was tragically fulfilled during Italy's surrender, when two revolutionary German gliding bombs plunged her into the Mediterranean Sea on her way to Malta to surrender to the Allies.

■ THE HISTORICAL CONTEXT: THE NAVAL ARMS RACE

Italy was in a singular position after the Great War. Unlike the other signatory powers of the Washington Naval Treaty (1922), the Regia Marina could afford to expand its fleet without having to scrap existing units. With just five operational battleships and a tonnage well below the imposed limits, Italy had carte blanche to modernize its navy.

However, French prudence in naval rearmament in the 1920s prompted Italy to focus mainly on heavy cruisers. The situation changed dramatically in 1932, when Paris launched the powerful *Dunkirk* Class ships, a clear response to threats from German pocket battleships. It was the spark that ignited a new arms race: Germany responded in turn by relaunching with the fearsome *Scharnhorst*, while Italy initiated the design of the futuristic *Littorio-class* ships.

▲ The *Roma*'s bow canopy shows a beautiful view of the battleship's two 381 forward towers (Photo: Ufficio Storico Marina Militare).

TECHNOLOGY AND INNOVATION: THE REVOLUTIONARY PROJECT

October 28, 1934 marked a historic date for Italian shipbuilding. In the prestigious shipyards of Trieste and Genoa, the keels of the *Vittorio Veneto* and *Littorio*, progenitors of a class that would set the standard. Italian designers managed to create a perfect balance between:

- Advanced armored protection;
- Above-average firepower;
- Outstanding speed performance.

The price to pay? A displacement that was close to 45,000 tons fully loaded, well beyond the limits of international treaties. It was in this context that the *R.N. Roma* was born, defined from the outset: national pride. In fact, the construction of the *Roma*, started in 1938 in Trieste, responded to precise strategic needs.

Admiral Cavagnari warned Mussolini that without new battleships, the Italian fleet would be outclassed by the combination of the two competing French and British navies. The launch in June 1940 coincided with Italy's entry into the war. Engineers brilliantly solved problems that had arisen during the twin ship trials, redefining the bow and upgrading the anti-aircraft armament. When she entered service two years later, the *Roma* represented excellence in Italian naval technology. Unfortunately, fate played against this magnificent unit by entailing an operational life marked by restrictions:

- Chronic fuel shortages drastically limited its operations;
- During the crucial convoy battle of August 1942, the *Roma* remained idle in Taranto;
- Continuous Allied bombardment forced the fleet into humiliating inactivity.

▲ The launch of the R.N. *Roma* took place in the Trieste shipyards on 9 June 1940. The hull was baptised by Princess Sofia Lanza Branciforte di Trabia, consort of the Governor of Rome, Gian Giacomo Borghese, in a rite that combined dynastic pomp and military might.

The most dramatic wartime episode occurred on June 5, 1943, when a wave of American B-17s hit La Spezia. An armor-piercing bomb ripped through the *Roma*'s hull, causing her to take on 2,350 tons of water. Despite the severe damage, engineers managed to bring her back into service after emergency repairs in Genoa shipyards. Like a phoenix the ship resurrected, but it was a short-lived affair.

Indeed, the *Roma* was coming to a tragic end: September 9, 1943, Italy signed the armistice the day before. As the Italian fleet headed toward Malta to surrender, the *Roma* was taken by surprise by an innovative German weapon: the FX-1400 guided bombs. Two precise hits sealed its fate. In just 25 minutes, the flagship of the Italian navy disappeared in the waves, taking 1,352 lives with it. Today, the wreck rests at a depth of about 400 meters in the Gulf of Asinara, a monument if together an underwater cemetery of the end of an era.

■ ORGANIZATION OF THIS VOLUME

This volume shows the entire history of the *R.N. Roma* and generically also of the *Littorio* classes to which the battleship belonged. It offers descriptions of its technical characteristics, operational history.

It shows the profile line from the side, from the top, the stern and bow views, summary tables, biographical sheets on the ship's important men, dozens of restored photos virtually all from the Central State Archives funds in PD, and many photos recolored with the colors of the time.

We have also attached several views of the 3D model in the camouflage livery of the bridge by artist "Cbhierro" who graciously grants its use in PD.

The part reserved for the ship model is particularly interesting: there are many *Roma* ship building kits on the market in different scales and sizes. There are also models made through the skill of model makers. We have resorted especially to the 1:350 scale model made by the good Roman model maker Matteo d'Aniello. We have also added other images by other well-known modelers such as Maurizio Maggi, Fulvio Faccio and others whom we thank for their great willingness.

▲ The 1:350 scale model of the R.N. *Roma* made by Roman modeller Maurizio Maggi, photographed by the author at an exhibition held in the castle of Urgnano (BG).

R.N. ROMA - LITTORIO CLASS 1938-1943

▲ This is the profile of the large Italian ship, over 240 metres long and heavily armed with a variety of artillery weapons. It is shown here in its original livery before the camouflage colours were added.

THE R.N. ROMA AND THE LITTORIO CLASS

ITALY'S UPGRADE OF LARGE BATTLESHIPS

After World War I, the Treaty of Washington (1922) imposed a "naval vacation," halting the construction of new warships and leading to the scrapping of some units, such as the used Italian *Caracciolo-class* battleships. Resuming construction, many navies preferred to modernize existing battleships (1908-1910), upgrading engines, armaments and firing systems. The Washington Conference (1921) was perhaps born more out of economic necessity than peace ideals, given the postwar financial disruption. The treaty limited battleship tonnage to 35,000 tons and gun caliber to 406 mm, freezing all new designs until 1931. Italy thus obtained parity with France and the opportunity to build 70,000 tons of ships, but made little use of this opportunity, concentrating mainly on cruisers and submarines.

In the 1920s, 23,000-ton battleships with 381-mm guns were studied, but the London Conference (1930) extended the "naval vacation" until 1936, without further reducing tonnage, thus causing intermediate plans to be abandoned.

However, as early as 1934, the major powers each resumed full freedom of action in armaments, and the General Staff of our Navy judged that 2 35,000-ton battleships alone albeit with the modernization of 4 units already in armament in World War I were not sufficient to face the eventual combined French and British forces in the Mediterranean; it therefore considered it necessary to build 2 more 35,000-ton battleships.

▲ The R.N. *Vittorio Veneto*, the first ship of the Littorio class as it prepares to enter Taranto's small sea at the height of the swing bridge.

▲ Admiral Angelo Iachino, commander of the Regia Marina's 1st Squadron, talks to the King of Italy, Victor Emmanuel III, on board the battleship *Littorio* during the latter's visit to Taranto, February 1942.

They had only slight modifications from their predecessors. One, *Roma*, was assigned in construction to Shipyards Riuniti dell'Adriatico, the other, *Impero*, to Ansaldo of Genoa; both were laid down in 1938. *Vittorio Veneto* and *Littorio* entered service in 1940, shortly before the start of hostilities, the *Roma* in 1942, and the *Impero*, after the armistice, was never completed. The most noticeable difference between the latter two and their predecessors was the line of the bow: *Roma* and *Impero* had a more raised forecastle, that is, a more pronounced leapfrog. The stern was of the cruiser type, slightly more rounded in the *Rome* and *Impero*. The 4 ships of the "*Littorio*" class had all other common features: notable was the arrangement of 3 rudders: one main axial and 2 auxiliary, secondary, between the inner and outer axles of the propellers, which were 4.

The relationship between the volume of the hull and the overall volume of the superstructures was very harmonious and gave such ships an aggressive appearance. The keep resumed the now proven pattern of the second series of "*Condottieri*" (*Muzio Attendolo, Eugenio di Savoia, Montecuccoli*).

In the center of the ship, 2 large funnels close together. The forward one had as an offshoot the machine gun firing direction platform. The higher forward mast was joined to the keep by 4 gangways, one of which served as a signal station. The lower aft mast rose from a structure abaft the funnels, which housed the aft command post and searchlights. A steerable catapult was arranged at the extreme stern for launching 3 aircraft, which were originally star-powered RO 43s, reconnaissance biplanes, hydroplanes "boot-shaped" that is, equipped with a large central float and 2 smaller ones under the wings and taller than the central one. On takeoff and ditching the plane kept itself balanced on the central one, while, when stationary, in the water, it remained slightly heeled resting on one of the side floats. At a later stage 2 of the RO 43 were replaced by King 2,000 fighters.

The strength of the armor was tested in May 1935 at the Cottrau coalfield in La Spezia. It proved capable of withstanding the impact of 406 mm armor-piercing shells fired from a distance of 24,000 m and that of 1,280 kg airplane bombs, of not excessive armor-piercing capacity but high explosive power, as well as capable of withstanding 835 kg armor-piercing bombs, both types of bombs with an impact velocity of 250 m/sec, i.e., the maximum natural fall speed (there were no rocket-propellant bombs then). Vertical

▲ Beautiful picture of the *Roma* in the final stages of readiness at the Monfalcone shipyard (summer 1942).

R.N. BATTLESHIP ROMA - LITTORIO CLASS 1938-1943

▲ Another profile of the battleship *Roma*, dated around 1942, in which the new livery with the new camouflage colours can be appreciated. A mock anchor was also painted at the bow.

protection in the central part of the ship, i.e., from the ammunition depot of tower No. 1 g.c., to the depot of tower No. 3 g.c. was provided by a 350 mm thick plate, not vertical, but converging downward with the median plane of the hull, so as to decrease the angle of impact of the shells, which was equivalent to a greater thickness of armor. The armor belt was reduced to 60 mm in the forward area and 100 mm in the aft area. A short distance from the armor belt was a 36-mm splinter bulkhead; another, also splinter, 24-mm bulkhead inclined in the opposite direction to the armor belt, arranged further inboard, also served as a support to the main armor deck. The armored redoubt was complemented by 2 armored transoms 210 mm thick at the bow and 290 mm thick at the stern. The transoms were respectively forward of the g.c. ammunition depot of tower No. 1 and aft of the g.c. depot of tower No. 3.

The project, headed by engineer Umberto Pugliese, combined technical innovations such as the decompressor cylinder underwater protection system. After two years of study and model testing, a displacement of about 40,000 tons was chosen, exceeding treaty limits. The optimal hulls were developed by the Shipyards Riuniti dell'Adriatico (C.R.D.A.), and construction began in 1934, marking the rebirth of the Italian battle fleet.

Roma, named after two earlier ships and the city of Rome, was the third *Littorio-class* battleship of the Italian Royal Navy. The construction of both *Roma* and her sister ship *Impero* was due to growing tensions around the world and the navy's fear that just two *Littorios*, even in company with older pre-World War I battleships, would not be enough to counter the British and French fleets in the Mediterranean in the event of a possible Franco-British alliance. Because *Roma* was laid down almost four years after the first two ships of the class, some minor improvements were made to the design, including the addition of an additional freeboard at the bow.

The *Roma* entered service in the Regia Marina on June 14, 1942, but a severe fuel shortage in Italy at that time prevented her deployment; instead, together with her sister ships *Vittorio Veneto* and *Littorio*, she was used to reinforce the anti-aircraft defenses of several Italian cities. In this role, she was severely damaged twice in June 1943 by bomber raids on La Spezia.

After repairs in Genoa, spent all of July and part of August, the *Roma* was deployed as Admiral Carlo Bergamini's flagship in a large battle group that eventually included the three *Littorios*, eight cruisers and eight destroyers. The battle group was supposed to attack Allied ships approaching Salerno to invade Italy (Operation *"Avalanche"*) on Sept. 9, 1943, but news of the armistice with the Allies on Sept. 8, 1943, led to the cancellation of the operation. Instead, the Italian fleet was ordered to sail for La Maddalena (Sardinia) and later Malta to surrender to the Allies.

▲ A well-known photograph of the R.N. battleship *Roma*, anchored in Trieste harbour on 21 August 1942 shortly before her transfer to Taranto to complete crew training and outfitting. It appears in its "standard" camouflage scheme, with dark grey polygonal panels on a light grey background; the white areas would later be recoloured in light grey by the end of 1942 (see profile image on opposite page).

HISTORICAL CONTEXT AND POLICY DECISIONS

Let us now take a step back and go all the way back to 1933. Until then, the fascist regime led by Benito Mussolini maintained a cautious attitude regarding naval rearmament. However, starting that year, significant changes marked the beginning of a new season for the Royal Navy. Two battleships of the *Conte di Cavour class* were undergoing a thorough modernization process, while the keel of two new battleships was laid: *Vittorio Veneto* and *Littorio*, in 1934.

In May 1935, the Italian Ministry of the Navy prepared an ambitious five-year shipbuilding plan, including four battleships, three aircraft carriers, four cruisers, fifty-five submarines and about forty smaller units. Within this strategic framework, Admiral Domenico Cavagnari proposed in December of that year the construction of two additional *Littorio-class* battleships. The goal was to counter a possible Franco-British naval alliance that could have quickly overtaken the Italian fleet in strength in the Mediterranean. Mussolini, initially hesitant, approved the planning of the two new units in January 1937, and in the following December the necessary funds were allocated. The new battleships were named *Roma* and *Impero*. Set against the criteria of evolution from her older sisters, *Roma* was designed with significant

▲ Italian sailors engaged with a sophisticated observation instrument on the new Italian battleships. This series of images refers to the light battleship *Giulio Cesare*. State Archives.

▲ The battleship *Roma* taken in full from above with the bow section in the foreground. Interesting to note the camouflage of the "half-armour" type painted on the ship's tower, before the modern camouflage of 1942.

R.N.ROMA DATA SHEET	
Type	Nave da battaglia - Classe Littorio
Shipyards	C.R.D.A San Marco Trieste
Laying - Launch - Completion	September 1938 / June 1940/ Sunk 9 September 1943
Displacement	44.050 t - 46.215 t full loaded
Measures (in meters)	Length: 240. Width: 33, Draught: 10,5
Propulsion	8 boilers, 4 Belluzzo turbines, 4 propellers Power: 130/140,000 hp
Maximum speed	31 knots (58 KM orari)
Autonomy	3920 miles at 20 knots (with 4000 t naphtha)
Crew	120 officers and 1,800 crew members
Onboard sensors	Radar EC3/ter «Gufo»
Gun armament	-9 × 381/50 Model 1934 (three triple turrets) -12 × 152/55 mm Model 1936 (four triple turrets) -4 × 120/40 mm (according to some sources Model 1891, others Model 1893) for illumination fire (four single mounts) -12 × 90/50 mm AA Model 1939 (twelve single turrets)
Deck machine guns	-16 × 37/54 mm AA Model 1932 (8 twin mounts) -4 × 37/54 mm AA Model 1939 (4 single mounts) -28 × 20/65 mm AA Model 1935 (14 twin mounts)
Armour	350 mm (vertical) 150/207 mm (horizontal above ammunition magazines) 350 mm (max. main artillery) 280 mm (max. secondary artillery) 260 mm (command tower)
Aircrafts	3 between IMAM Ro.43 and Reggiane Re.2000 aircraft

improvements: a raised bow for a greater freeboard and a refined waterline derived from the experience gained with *Vittorio Veneto*. She was also equipped with thirty-two 20 mm/65 Breda guns, instead of the original twenty-four.

■ **TECHNICAL AND DESIGN FEATURES**

Description

The battleship *Roma* had an overall length of 240.68 meters (789 feet 8 inches), a maximum breadth of 32.82 meters (107 feet 8 inches) and a draft of 9.6 meters (31 feet 6 inches). The standard displacement was 40,992 long tons (41,650 metric tons), a figure that exceeded the limits imposed by the Washington Naval Treaty (35,000 long tons), although that treaty had already lapsed by the time the keel was laid. Fully loaded for war employment, *Roma* reached a displacement of 45,485 long tons (46,215 metric tons).

Propulsion was provided by four Belluzo reduction steam turbines, fed by eight liquid-fueled Yarrow boilers, capable of developing a total of 128,000 horsepower (95,000 kW). This enabled the ship to reach a maximum speed of 30 knots (about 56 km/h), with an operating range of 3,920 nautical miles (7,260 km) at a cruising speed of 20 knots (37 km/h).

The crew consisted of between 1,830 and 1,950 men. A catapult was installed aft for launching reconnaissance aircraft, and the air equipment included up to three IMAM Ro.43 seaplanes or Reggiane Re.2000 fighters.

The design of the class was overseen by Naval Engineer Inspector General Umberto Pugliese. Ships of this class represent one of the earliest examples of battleships with a displacement of more than 35,000 tons, a threshold set by the naval treaty then in force. This limit was largely exceeded-as had already been the case with the Zara-class heavy cruisers-in order to meet operational and design requirements deemed a priority. In fact, according to a confidential document prepared by the Undersecretariat of the Navy, the internal limit set was 40,000 tons.

After the launching of the first two units of the class (*Littorio* and *Vittorio Veneto*) in 1934, the international situation-worsened by the conflicts in Ethiopia and Spain-induced the Italian government to strengthen the naval rearmament program. Thus, in 1938, the last two units were set: *Roma* and her twin sister *Impero*.

PROPULSION SYSTEMS AND TECHNICAL EQUIPMENT

The propulsive heart of the *Roma* was a refined steam-powered complex, the result of the most advanced Italian naval engineering of the time. The apparatus comprised four turbo-reducer units powered by steam produced by eight Yarrow-type boilers, adapted to Regia Marina standards and fuelled by naphtha. In these boilers, water was preheated by an ingenious system that used waste heat from exhaust gases, thus optimizing overall thermal efficiency.

The engine system was protected with great care: each boiler was enclosed in an independent armored cylinder, while armored gratings safeguarded the openings near the funnels. This protection was harmoniously integrated with the ship's upper armor and triple bottom structure, which extended into the armored citadel area.

▲ Flag-raising ceremony on the wooden-planked aft deck.

The power developed by the entire apparatus reached 130,000 horsepower, ensuring a theoretical maximum speed of 31 knots. Under operating conditions, at a cruising speed of 20 knots, the range was limited to 3,380 nautical miles: a modest figure compared to counterpart units of other navies, which effectively confined the *Roma*'s employment to the Mediterranean sphere.

The system provided for an interesting emergency solution: in the event of a failure of one of the turbo-reducers, it was possible to direct superheated steam to the high-pressure turbine, thus achieving an overload power of 36,000 horsepower per unit. According to the logbook kept at the Navy Historical Office, in tests at full power on August 21, 1942, the *Roma* reached and maintained an effective speed of 29.2 knots for one hour.

Power transmission was via four drive axles connected to as many three-blade propellers-two central and two side propellers. The ship was steered by a main rudder located aft, exactly in the central propeller stream, flanked by two auxiliary side rudders, intended for emergency steering and located in the side propeller stream.

The air component, though limited, was significant: the ship could embark up to three aircraft, all belonging to the Regia Aeronautica, as the Navy was not allowed direct ownership of aircraft. In normal service these were IMAM Ro.43 reconnaissance seaplanes, but from the summer of 1943 two Reggiane Re.2000 fighters in catapult version were also embarked.

For the recovery of seaplanes, the *Roma* was equipped with two cranes, although the complexity of the operations-which required the ship to come to a complete stop-made it more practical to direct the aircraft to Allied airfields, an unavoidable necessity in the case of fighters. The Reggiane Re.2000s came from the Naval Battle Forces Air Reserve Squadron, consisting of eight aircraft, six of which were operational at the time of the armistice. One of these was actually aboard the *Roma* at the time of its departure for La Maddalena.

Among the technological equipment on board, it is worth mentioning the EC3/ter "Owl" radar, developed by SAFAR of Milan, a rare example of the advanced electronics employed by the Italian Navy in those years.

▲ Another beautiful picture of the battleship *Roma* in which the ship's elaborate camouflage appears in all its geometry. Small picture: a rare image of the EC3/ter "Gufo" radar developed by SAFAR in Milan for the Navy.

R.N. BATTLESHIP ROMA - LITTORIO CLASS 1938-1943

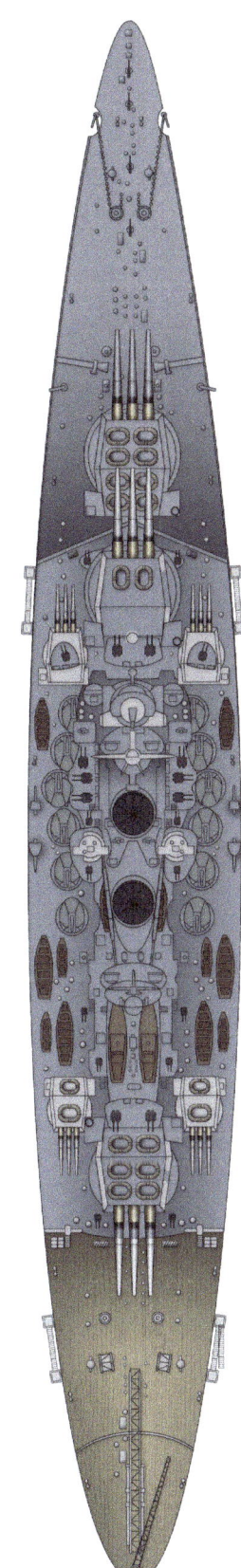 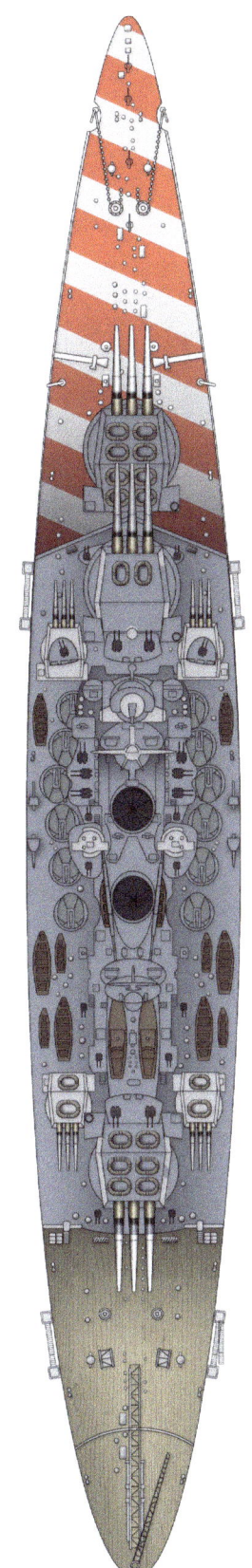

▲ Two views from above of the *Roma* battleship's profile: the first without red and white stripes precedes the camouflage solution. The second refers to the livery adopted in 1942.

R.N. BATTLESHIP ROMA - LITTORIO CLASS 1938-1943

▲ R.N. battleship *Roma*, view of the bow.

ARMAMENT

The *Roma*'s main armament represented the pinnacle of Italian naval power of the period, a perfect synthesis of brute force and technical precision. The battleship's offensive core consisted of nine 381 mm, model 1934, 50-caliber guns distributed in three electrically operated trunnion turrets: two located forward and one aft. These giants of naval artillery were capable of launching armor-piercing projectiles weighing 885 kg or explosives weighing 774 kg, with an initial speed of 850 and 870 meters per second, respectively. Allowable elevation ranged from a minimum of -5°30' to a maximum of 36°, allowing a theoretical maximum range of as much as 44,000 meters. However, under real operating conditions and effective direct fire, this range was reduced to between 28,000 and 30,000 meters.

The construction of these towers was entrusted to two of Italy's leading war industries of the time: the three cannons of the forward tower were made by Ansaldo, while the remaining six gun ports, distributed between the aft tower and the second forward tower, came out of the factories of O.T.O. (Odero Terni Orlando), a testament to national industrial cooperation in the construction of these impressive war machines.

To complement the 381-mm pieces in the antiaircraft and antiaircraft roles, the *Roma* was equipped with substantial secondary armament: twelve 152-mm long 55-gauge guns, model 1936, arranged in four trunnion turrets. These weapons, although designed for countering enemy light units, were also usable for antiaircraft barrage because of their good elevation and rapidity of fire.

For defense against air attacks, the ship had twelve 90/50 mm guns, installed in single drums. These guns, with manual loading, were dual type-that is, they could be used against both air and naval targets-and reached a maximum elevation of 75°. The range against surface targets varied, according to sources, between 13,000 and 15,548 meters, while the antiaircraft tangency (i.e., the maximum altitude attainable by a projectile) ranged between 9,000 and 10,500 meters.

In addition, the ship was equipped with four 120/40 mm pieces used for night illuminating fire, and a large automatic artillery battery for close defense: twenty 37/54 mm Breda guns (in eight twin and four single installations) and at least twenty-eight 20/65 mm machine guns arranged in fourteen twin installations. Some sources, however, indicate a slightly higher number, up to thirty-two machine guns

▲ The two gigantic bow towers of the *Roma* with 381 mm guns of the 1934 model, the battleship's true offensive hammer.

distributed in sixteen twin installations, a sign of variations over time or divergences in coeval technical documents.

Experience with sister units *Littorio* and *Vittorio Veneto* led to significant improvements in the fire direction system on the *Roma*. The antiaircraft control panels were upgraded, enabling the effective engagement of targets up to 14,000 meters away and 8,000 meters in altitude - higher than the limits of previous ships of the class, which stopped at 12,000 meters and 6,000 meters, respectively.

This armament apparatus, together with sophisticated fire control equipment, made the *Roma* one of the most modern and fearsome battleships of the era, although its capabilities were not allowed to fully express themselves due to the dramatic circumstances that marked its short operational career.

▲ Italian sailor observing the horizon from a station on the new Italian battleships. This series of images refers to the light battleship *Giulio Cesare*. State Archives.

R.N. BATTLESHIP ROMA - LITTORIO CLASS 1938-1943

▲ R.N. battleship *Roma*, stern view.

▲ Italian sailors engaged with a sophisticated observation instrument on the new Italian battleships. This series of images refers to the light battleship *Giulio Cesare*. State Archives.

▲ Beautiful view in length of the battleship *Roma*, probably in the port of Trieste. State Archives.

PROTECTION

The defensive system of the battleship *Roma* represented one of the most advanced examples of Italian naval engineering of the period, the result of careful planning aimed at ensuring the unit's maximum survival even under the most intense fire. The central core of the ship, comprised between the forward and aft towers, consisted of an armored citadel - the most heavily protected part - designed to safeguard the vital organs of the vessel: ammunition stores, firing stations, engine apparatus and command rooms.

Above, this citadel was covered by horizontal armor that varied in thickness: 100 mm in the aft area, tapering gradually to 70 mm toward the bow. In the vertical plane, protection was provided by a strong armor belt with a maximum thickness of 350 mm, sloping 15° inward - a choice designed to improve the deflection capacity of enemy shells. This main armor extended well below the waterline, providing protection even against shots that tried to hit the hull underwater. At both ends of the ship, the thickness of the belt was gradually reduced to 60 mm.

Inside the hull, parallel to the outer armor, was a double splinter bulkhead: the first 36 mm thick, followed by a second 24 mm thick. This double layer was intended to contain any fragments that penetrated beyond the main armor, reducing the risk of fire or explosion in the inner compartments. The organization of the compartmentalization and the ship's internal balancing gave the *Roma* considerable stability and buoyancy, even in case of severe damage from torpedoes or mines, as demonstrated in cases where her sister units - *Littorio* and *Vittorio Veneto* - managed to return to port despite repeated hits received in battle.

Underwater protection was provided by the innovative Pugliese cylinder system, a solution devised by general and naval engineer Umberto Pugliese, intended to provide an effective response to the torpedo threat. This system consisted of large hollow cylinders with a diameter of 3.80 meters and a length of about 120 meters, installed inside a cavity along the hull sides, between the outer and inner hulls. These cavities were filled with liquids-usually water or naphtha-that acted as a dissipative medium in the event of an underwater explosion.

▲ The battleship *Roma* in 1942, with sailors engaged in on-board work, including the restoration and cleaning of the sides.

UMBERTO PUGLIESE

Umberto Pugliese (Naples, 1880 - Rome, 1961) was a leading figure in Italian naval engineering and one of the protagonists of the technical renaissance of the Royal Navy in the early 20th century.

An engineer and Naval Engineer officer, he reached the rank of inspector general, distinguishing himself by his innovative vision and deep sense of patriotic duty.

His fame is mainly linked to the conception of the underwater protection system known as the "**Pugliese Cylinder**", an original and ambitious solution designed to protect warships from underwater explosions caused by mines and torpedoes. This system was adopted in *Littorio-class* battleships (*Littorio*, *Vittorio Veneto*, *Roma* and *Impero*), among the most modern battleships of the time.

THE PUGLIESE SYSTEM

The principle on which it was based was as simple as it was ingenious: between the outer broadside and the inner hull was a compartment filled with water or naphtha, inside which ran a large hollow metal cylinder, about 3.80 meters in diameter and up to 120 meters long. In the event of an underwater explosion, the shock wave would compress and deform the cylinder, dissipating some of the energy of the explosion and thus protecting the inner hull.

Although the system proved to be theoretically sound, in practice it was not always as effective as intended, mainly due to construction limitations and the increasing power of enemy underwater weapons. Nevertheless, Pugliese's conceptual contribution remains an example of Italian naval engineering's attempt to compete at the highest international level in an era of rapid technological and warfare evolution.

CAREER AND PERSECUTION

Pugliese was also director general of Naval Construction at the Ministry of the Navy and played a central role in the modernization of the fleet in the 1930s. He was also a fervent advocate of integrated ship design, always trying to reconcile technical, operational and industrial needs.

In 1938, with the promulgation of the fascist racial laws, Pugliese, who was of Jewish descent, was forced to leave active service despite his very high competence and valor demonstrated. It was not until after the war that he was able to fully regain his rightful role and honor.

With the birth of the Italian Republic, he was reinstated in his rights and welcomed with respect in the academic and technical world.

LEGACY

Umberto Pugliese is remembered not only for his technical ingenuity, but also for his moral integrity and dedication to the service of the country. His name remains linked to an era in which the Italian Navy sought, albeit amid limitations and contradictions, to renew itself profoundly. His work represents one of the highest moments of national naval engineering in the 20th century.

▲ The Pugliese system can be clearly seen in this interesting photo of the hull being worked on, where a huge cylinder was placed at the height of the central third of the side to act as a shield against torpedoes and mines.

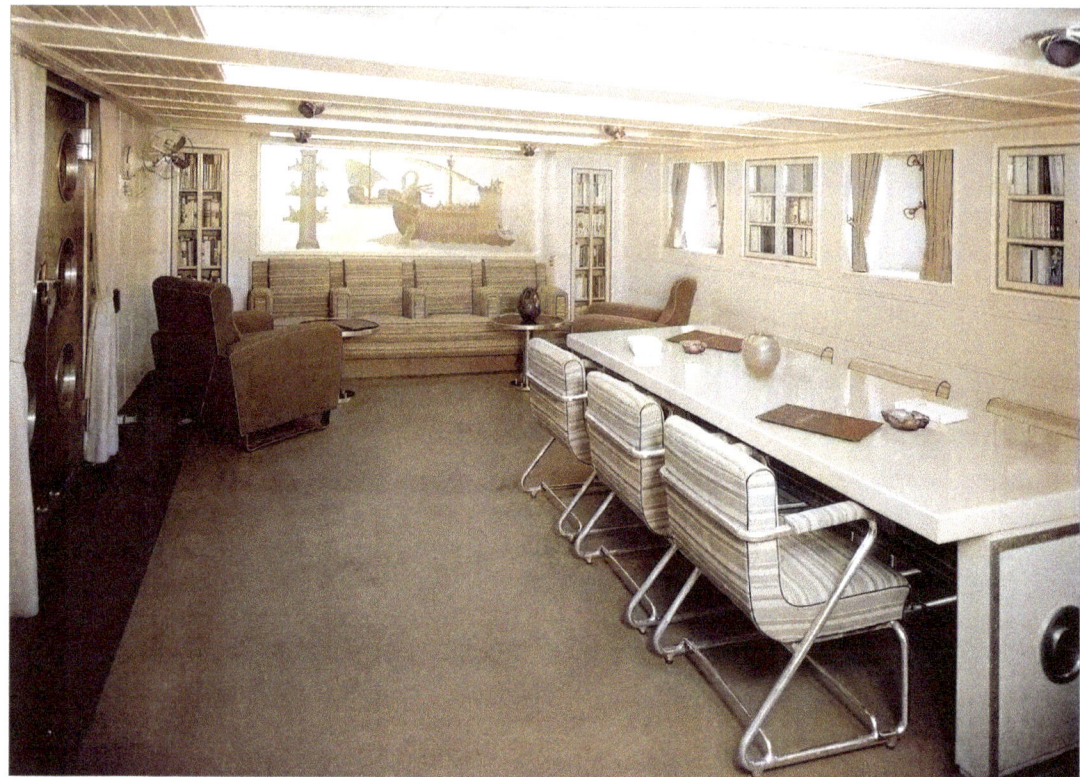

▲▼ Pictures of the ship's interior, detailed and extremely modern. Command meeting rooms, accommodation and library can be seen on the page above and the one opposite.

Should a mine or torpedo hit the ship, the shock wave would propagate through these liquid compartments until it reached the cylinder, which would deform, crush, or shatter, absorbing much of the explosive energy. This controlled deformation mechanism was intended to limit the transmission of the wave to the interior living spaces, thus reducing the severity of structural damage to the main hull.

Although in practice the Pugliese system proved less effective than hoped-especially in the face of explosives of increasing power-it remains a testimony to the Italian willingness to come up with original and courageous solutions in the field of naval defense, at a time when the technological superiority of battleships was still considered the foundation of maritime power.

■ CONSTRUCTION AND ENTRY INTO SERVICE

Construction of the *Roma*, the third of the mighty *Littorio-class* battleships, began on September 18, 1938, at the prestigious Shipyards Riuniti dell'Adriatico (CRDA) at the San Marco shipyard in Trieste. The ship's launching took place on June 9, 1940, in a climate now fraught with wartime tensions: it was celebrated with solemnity just one day before Italy's declaration of war on the United Kingdom and France.

The hull was christened by Princess Sofia Lanza Branciforte of Trabia, consort of the Governor of *Rome*, Gian Giacomo Borghese, in a rite that combined dynastic pomp and military might.

Although she was launched almost in parallel with her twin sister *Impero*, the outfitting of the *Roma* took an additional two months, due to modifications to the bow introduced as a result of experiences gained during the *Littorio*'s first sea trials. The urgency of operational needs even led to an unexpected detour in the completion process: on March 28, 1941, during the Battle of Cape Matapan, an aerial torpedo damaged a propeller shaft of the *Vittorio Veneto*. To expedite its repair, *Rome* was urgently towed to the Monfalcone Shipyard on April 4 to temporarily surrender one of its axles, which was later reinstalled on the *Vittorio Veneto*. Immediately thereafter, the unit was returned to Trieste on the night of April 17-18 to continue outfitting.

CARLO BERGAMINI (1888-1943)

THE ADMIRAL WHO FELL WITH THE SHIP *ROMA*

Carlo Bergamini was one of the Regia Marina's most distinguished admirals, a protagonist in both world wars. His career, marked by courage and dedication, ended tragically with the sinking of the battleship *Roma*, in which he lost his life along with 1,393 crewmen. For his valor, he was awarded the Gold Medal for Military Valor.

Born in San Felice sul Panaro, in the province of Modena, Bergamini trained at the Livorno Naval Academy. He became an ensign and served on the battleship *Regina Elena* and later participated in the Italo-Turkish War aboard the cruiser *Vettor Pisani*.

Promoted to lieutenant-lieutenant, he assumed the role of firing director on the cruiser *Pisa* during World War I. He distinguished himself in the defense of Valona (1916) and the bombardment of Durres (1918), an action that earned him the Silver Medal for Military Valor.

After the war, Bergamini took command of a torpedo boat and later became director of gunnery on the *Doria*. His expertise in weapon systems led him to the General Directorate of Arms and Naval Armaments of the Ministry of the Navy (1929-1931).

After further assignments on various units, he was recalled to the Ministry in 1937, contributing to the technological development of the fleet.

THE ADMIRAL AT WAR

Promoted rear admiral (1938) and then division admiral (1939), he assumed command of the 5th Naval Division, leading the battleships *Conte di Cavour* and *Giulio Cesare*.

During World War II, he commanded the 9th Division and participated in the Battle of Cape Teulada (1940) aboard the *Vittorio Veneto*, earning the Military Order of Savoy.

In 1943, he became commander in chief of the Italian battle fleet, with insignia on the *Roma*, a ship for which he had personally designed the firing systems.

OPERATION SIGMA AND THE LAST DAYS

In August 1943, a daring attack against Allied bases in Palermo and Bona was proposed to him, but Bergamini expressed doubts about the operation, which was eventually canceled.

Meanwhile, the situation in Italy was becoming increasingly critical. After the September 8 armistice, the Italian fleet was ordered to surrender to the Allies. While sailing to Malta, the *Roma* was hit and sunk by German bombers on September 9, 1943. Bergamini chose to remain at her post, sharing the fate of her crew.

LEGACIES AND AWARDS

In addition to the Gold Medal for Military Valor, Bergamini is remembered as a capable and resolute officer, a symbol of dedication to duty to the point of extreme sacrifice. The Italian Navy named a frigate after him, keeping alive the memory of a hero of the sea.

The *Roma* made her first independent sailing on November 9, 1941, although still lacking the missing axle. She reached Venice, where that component was restored, and then returned to the Trieste shipyard on December 14. From the launching stage, the unit's command was entrusted to Captain Adone Del Cima, who closely followed all phases of its completion, which was completed during the first four months of 1942. In May of that year, the ship carried out sea trials, maneuvering in the Gulf of Trieste under the protection of a specially prepared naval escort.

Finally, on June 14, 1942-exactly two years after her launch-the *Roma* officially entered service in the Regia Marina. However, the changed strategic conditions of the conflict prevented the ship from taking part in significant naval engagements against the Royal Navy.

On August 22 the *Roma* reached Taranto, where she was framed in the 9th Naval Division, along with her sisters *Littorio* and *Vittorio Veneto*. Following the Allied landing in North Africa (Operation Torch), the division was ordered to transfer from Taranto to Naples on November 11, which ended on November 13 without damage, despite interception by the British submarines *HMS Umbra* and *HMS Turbulent*, whose torpedoes missed their target.

On December 4, 1942, during a violent bombardment of the port of Naples by Allied forces, the *Roma* and the other battleships of the IX Division managed to escape unharmed, in contrast to the VII Division, which suffered heavy losses: the cruiser *Attendolo* was sunk and the other units damaged. As a result of this attack, Supermarina ordered the IX Division to be moved to La Spezia, a transfer that was carried out between December 6 and 7 without incident.

▲ The forward towers with their six 381 mm cannons represented the most modern calibre in use in the Italian wartime navy.

R.N. BATTLESHIP ROMA - LITTORIO CLASS 1938-1943

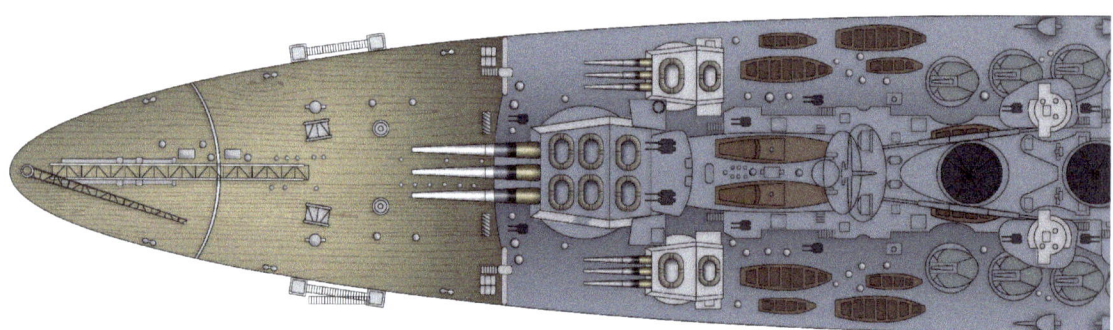

▲ Large overall profile of the battleship *Roma*, dated around 1942, in which the new livery with the new camouflage colours appeared.

R.N. BATTLESHIP ROMA - LITTORIO CLASS 1938-1943

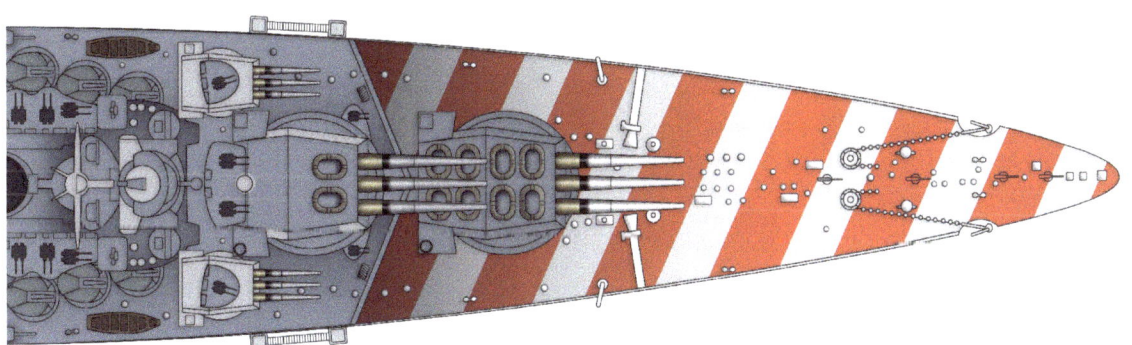

▲ In the original version, and this can be seen in the photo on page 13, a mock anchor was also painted on the bow.

In the first half of 1943, operational activity of the three battleships was kept to a minimum, partly due to fuel shortages and the growing air threat. Between Feb. 12 and Feb. 20, *Roma* underwent hull cleaning at the dockyard in Genoa. It was at La Spezia, which had meanwhile become an operational base, that the *Roma* faced its first serious Anglo-American air attacks: on April 14, 1943, 208 British four-engine bombers struck the *Littorio*, severely damaging its number two tower. The damage was repaired by May, however.

A second massive bombardment by 173 aircraft followed on April 19, sinking the destroyer *Alpino*, but leaving the three battleships relatively unscathed. But on June 5, in the midst of a daylight raid conducted by 118 USAAF B-17s, *Roma* was indirectly hit: two 2,000-pound bombs exploded in the water close to the bow, causing two serious 6×5 and 8×5-meter leaks on the starboard and port sides. The ship embarked 2,350 tons of water, heeled slightly to port, and the bow rested on the shallow bottom of the harbor. The *Vittorio Veneto* also suffered damage, so much so that for several weeks the *Littorio* remained the only operational battleship.

While *the Vittorio Veneto* was repaired in time to return to service in a little more than a month, the *Roma came* under further attack: on the night of June 24 she was hit by two more bombs, which, however, did not cause any flaws in the hull. The severity of the earlier injuries, however, made it necessary to enter dry dock and transfer to Genoa, which took place on July 1. It was not until August 13 that *Roma* could again be said to be combat ready, rejoining the squadron.

A few days later, on September 8, 1943, in the turbulent scenario that saw the announcement of the armistice with the Allies, Admiral Carlo Bergamini - commander in chief of the Naval Battle Forces - assumed command directly from the *Roma*, which became his flagship. It would be the final act in his operational history.

▲ Two pictures of the R.N. *Roma* in the port of La Spezia. The one above, particularly dramatic, shows the daytime air attack, carried by dozens of USAF B-17s, which caused serious damage to the battleship and necessitated restoration work at the dry dock.

THE END OF A GREAT SHIP

■ **THE SINKING OF THE BATTLESHIP ROMA**

A tragedy in Italian naval history

September 8, 1943 marked a dramatic turning point for the Italian Royal Navy. The battleship *Roma*, flagship of the battle fleet under the command of Admiral Carlo Bergamini, was anchored in La Spezia, ready to set sail to counter the Allied landing at Salerno scheduled for the following day.
However, around 5 p.m., Bergamini learned from civilian radio broadcasts the shocking news of the armistice between Italy and the Allies, which was made official at 7:40 p.m. by Marshal Pietro Badoglio's proclamation. The armistice clauses mandated the immediate surrender of the Italian fleet to the Allies, with orders to move promptly to designated ports, including Bona in Algeria and Malta.

Ships were supposed to raise black panels on their flagpoles and draw black circles on their decks as a sign of surrender. Bergamini, furious at not having been informed in advance, threatened to self-sink the fleet or resign. Eventually, he reluctantly accepted Supermarina's orders: the naval squadron was to initially reach La Maddalena, Sardinia, where King Victor Emmanuel III and the government were scheduled to move. Although British Admiral Andrew Cunningham suggested setting sail at sunset to avoid air attacks, Bergamini, underestimating the threat of the Luftwaffe, did not set the fleet sail until 03:00 on September 9.

With Roma leading the way, battleships *Vittorio Veneto* and *Italia (formerly Littorio)* also sailed, as well as cruisers, destroyers and torpedo boats. The formation rejoined off Genoa with a second naval group, consisting of the cruisers *Garibaldi, Duca d'Aosta and Duca degli Abruzzi*. While underway, Supermarina ordered a response to any German attacks, but the lack of air cover proved to be a serious handicap. Four Macchi M.C.202 fighters took off from Olbia to escort the fleet, but failed to locate it. Around noon, Bergamini received news that La Maddalena had been occupied by the Germans. Supermarina then ordered

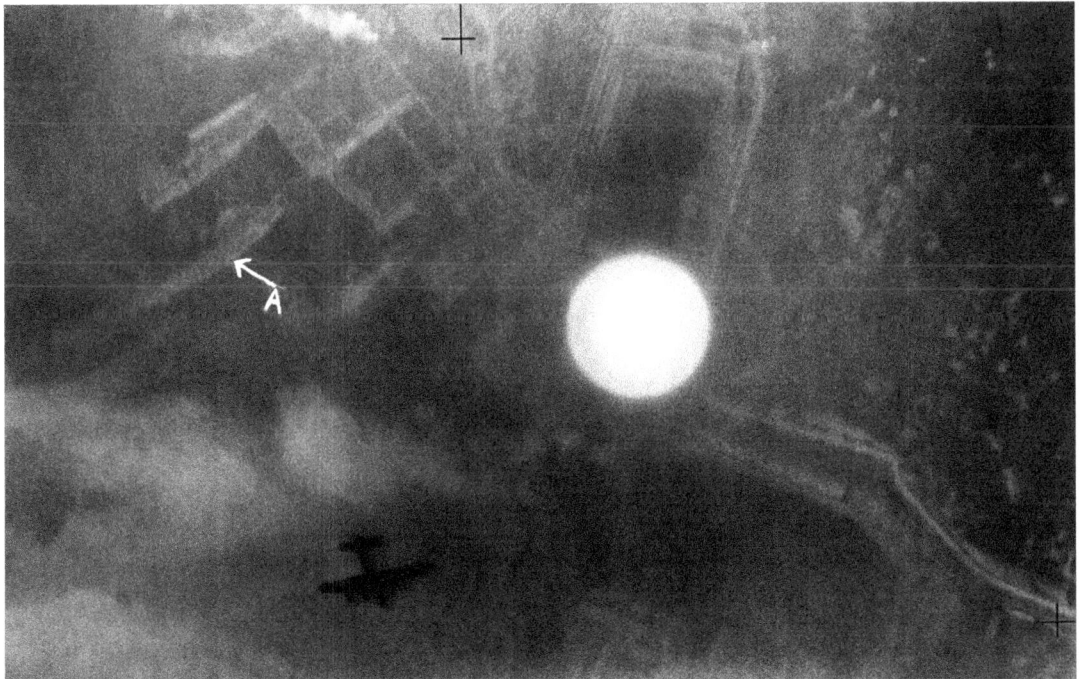

▲ Before 8 September 1943, the *Roma*'s operational history was characterised above all by its attack at anchor in the port of La Spezia, as recalled by this historic photo, taken by a British Avro Lancaster aircraft. Indicated with an A, the silhouette of the *Roma* at anchor in its quay.

him to reverse course and head for Bona. During the maneuver, the formation arranged itself in a new line, with the destroyers in the lead and the *Roma* in the rear.

The attack of the Luftwaffe: the fate of the Battleship Rome

At 15:10 on September 9, 1943, as the Italian naval squadron was sailing off the island of Asinara, twenty-eight Dornier Do 217K bombers of the Luftwaffe's Kampfgeschwader 100 appeared in the sky at high altitude. Taking off from Istres airport near Marseille, the planes arrived in three successive waves, the first of which had taken flight shortly after 2 p.m. with a specific objective: to strike the Italian battleships. Keeping in level flight, the bombers dropped tapered devices, whose bright trail, seen from the enormous altitude, was initially mistaken by Italian crews for a recognition signal. In reality, these were the deadly Ruhrstahl SD 1400 remote-controlled bombs, named "Fritz X" by the Allies.

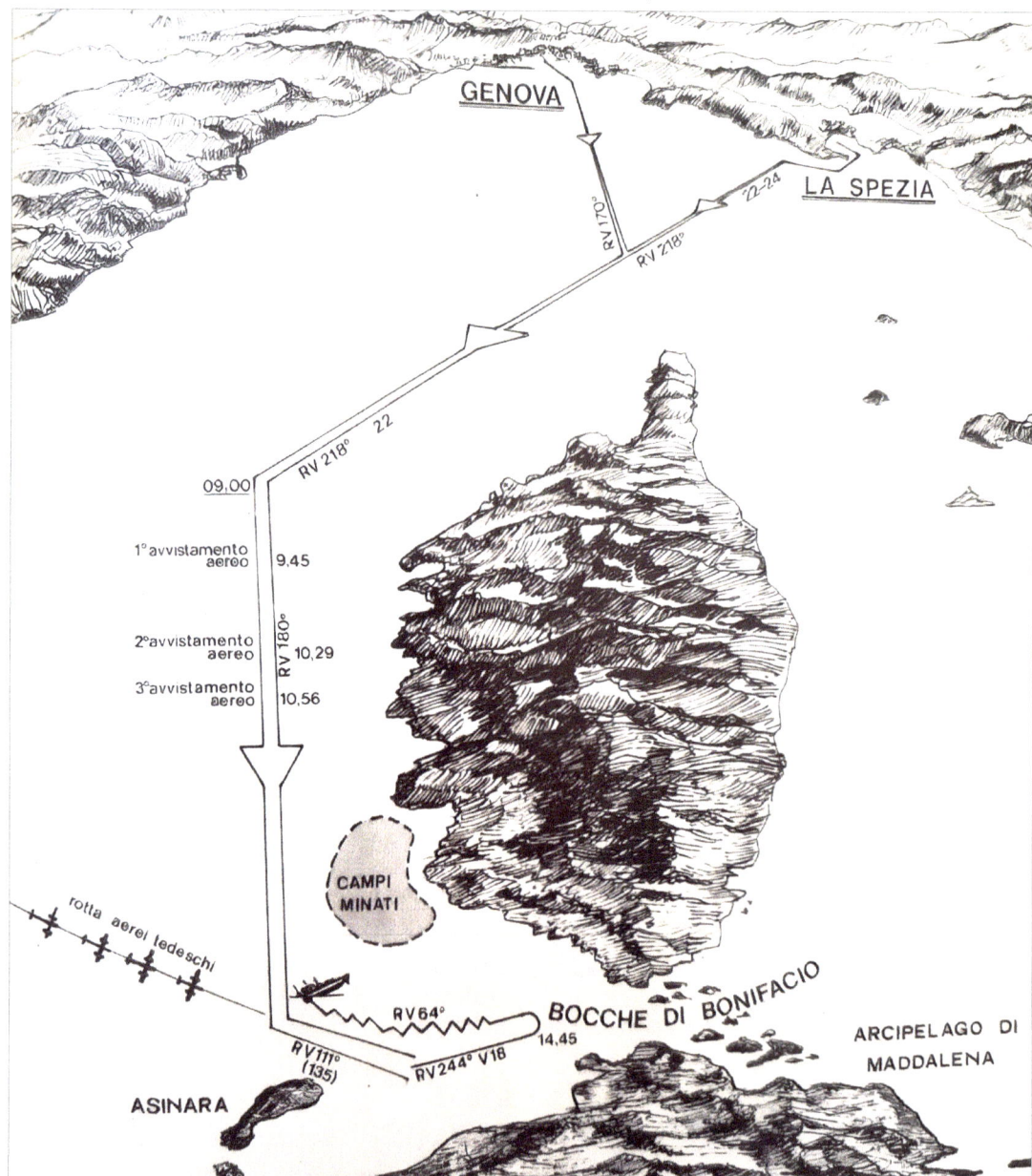

▲ A chart of the time that reconstructs the last sailing of the *Roma* together with a large part of the Italian fleet destined to sail to Malta for the final surrender, instead meeting a fatal fate near Asinara.

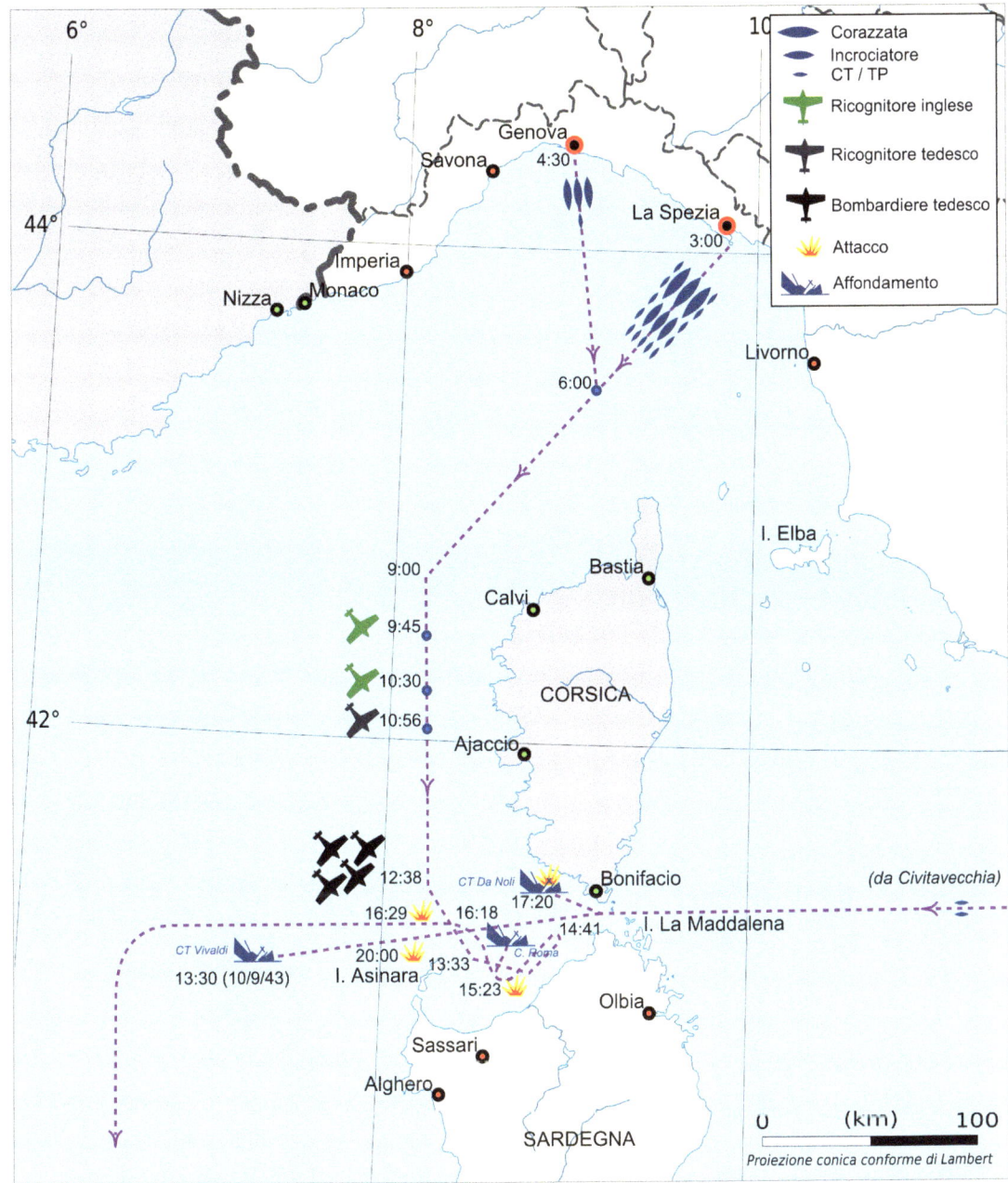

▲ A more modern reconstruction of the dramatic navigation of the Italian fleet in that fateful September 1943, with the clash between Corsica and Sardinia against a formation of German bombers.

The lethal technology of Fritz X bombs

These bombs, designed to penetrate the strongest armor, were dropped from an altitude of at least 5,000 meters, gaining devastating speed as they fell. What made them particularly dangerous was their radio guidance system, which allowed operators aboard aircraft to correct their trajectory in flight. The only way to counter them would have been to jam the radio frequencies, but the Royal Navy of the time had no such countermeasures. In addition, the operational altitude of the Dorniers (about 6,500 meters) rendered Italian flak ineffective. The 90/50 mm guns, while among the best available, could not rise above 75°, leaving the German planes beyond their reach. Major Bernhard Joppe, commander of the formation, stated on this subject in an interview in the 1970s, "I did not know the calibers of the Italian flak, but I knew that they could fire up to about 4,000 meters. And we were flying at least 5,000 meters, the optimum altitude for directing bombs. We saw many shells explode below us, but always at a safe distance, without any damage."

THE BEGINNING OF THE ATTACK

Because of strict neutrality provisions, Italian ships opened fire only when it became clear that planes were dropping bombs. However, the anti-aircraft, forced to fire at maximum elevation, succeeded only in creating a barrage that proved ineffective.

This is the sequence of events:

- 15:30: the first German Fritz X was directed toward the cruiser *Eugene of Savoy*, but fell 50 meters away without causing damage.

- A few minutes later, a second bomb exploded very close to the stern of the battleship *Italia*, damaging its power plant and blocking its main rudder. The crew managed to maintain control of the ship using auxiliary rudders.

The fatal blow to the Battleship Rome

Then it was the turn of the *Roma*, flagship of the fleet:

- 15:42 - Oberleutnant Heinrich Schmetz centered the battleship between the fifth and sixth starboard anti-aircraft towers. The device pierced the hull and exploded underwater, causing a breach but without immediately catastrophic effects.

- 3:50 p.m. - A second, far more devastating blow struck the *Roma* in the bow, on the port side, between the command tower and the 381 mm and 152 mm main towers, causing the beginning of the end of the Italian fleet's flagship.

▲ Flag-raising ceremony on the aft deck with the ship moored in Trieste.

▲ Historic image of the moment when Roma received the decisive blow that would lead to the subsequent sinking.

BATTLESHIP ROMA WWII

The explosion set off a chain reaction:

- The boilers flooded, stranding the ship.

- The ammunition stores deflagrated, blowing up tower number 2 (1,500 tons of steel hurled into the sea).

- The command tower was hit by a blaze of heat so intense that it deformed and disintegrated, instantly killing Admiral Carlo Bergamini, Commander Adone Del Cima and most of the general staff.

- A column of fire rose 400-1,500 meters, forming a mushroom cloud similar to that of nuclear explosions.

The Roma, broken in two, capsized and sank within minutes (precisely at 4:11 p.m.), dragging 1,352 men with her. Those in the stern had no chance: fifty sailors, already about to throw themselves overboard, were pulverized by the explosion. The survivors, many of them severely burned, were recovered by escorting destroyers.

The last attack on Italy

At 4:29 p.m., the battleship *Italia* was hit again, this time by a PC 1400X bomb, which opened a 7.5 x 6-meter gash in her below the waterline. Despite embarking 1,066 tons of water, the ship managed to stay afloat and continue sailing.

At the same times a British Martin B-26 scout plane, piloted by Lieutenant Colonel Herbert Law-Wright, took a dramatic picture of *Roma* broken in two, while all the Italian ships continued to fire at the German planes.

Conclusion

The Luftwaffe attack demonstrated the lethal effectiveness of guided bombs and the impotence of ships without air cover. The loss of the *Roma* marked one of the Italian Navy's most tragic moments in World War II, an event that is still remembered today as a symbol of courage and sacrifice, but also with much sorrow.

▲ The deadly German Ruhrstahl SD 1400 Fritz X bomb, pictured here at the Royal Air Force museum in London (UK). Courtesy by Kogo Wiki cc1.

The rescue and internment in the Balearic Islands

The destroyers *Mitragliere, Carabiniere* and other units stopped to retrieve the shipwrecked men, saving 622 men. Without contact with the rest of the fleet, the commander of these units, Giuseppe Marini decided to head for Mahón, in the Spanish Balearic Islands, hoping for neutral help. However, Spanish authorities interned ships and crews. The survivors of the *Roma* and other units then spent months in captivity, while the wounded were admitted to local hospitals.

The finding of the wreck

For decades, the exact location of the wreck of the *Roma* remained a mystery. It was not until 2012 that engineer Guido Gay, using an ROV, located the remains of the battleship more than 1,000 meters (more traditionally specified as 400 meters) deep in the canyon of Castelsardo. The wreck, broken into several sections, still retains cannons and recognizable structures, confirming the ship's tragic end. The sinking of the *Roma* still represents one of the most dramatic episodes in Italian naval history, a symbol of the chaos that followed the armistice of September 8, 1943. Today the wreck is an underwater shrine, a silent testimony to the sacrifice of those men and the end of an era.

▲ The heroic Admiral Carlo Bergamini, commander of the fleet on board the battleship *Roma*, was among the first to perish; here he is pictured in a period photo decorating a naval officer. Today, in his honour, the Italian Navy has dedicated a ship to him, the modern missile-launching frigate that bears his name.

▲ Another image of the beautiful ship, pride of the Italian fleet.

▲ Quiet moment during navigation (in this case on board the battleship *Giulio Cesare*) showing a scene similar to what it must have been like on board on that fateful day before the arrival of the German planes.

THE AIRCRAFT OF THE BATTLESHIP ROMA

THE AVIATION OF THE ITALIAN NAVY

At the outbreak of World War II, the Ro.43 was the only seaplane embarked on the Regia Marina, with 42 operational units. Inadequate as a fighter (armed only with two machine guns), it was improved in a second version, growing to 194 units, but remaining relegated to reconnaissance and observation. The complex recovery operations, carried out while the ship was stationary, prompted a preference to return to the waterfront, limiting each aircraft to one mission per sailing.

Italian air cover proved insufficient compared to the Royal Navy, as demonstrated in the night of Taranto (1940) and the Battle of Cape Matapan (1941), where the lack of aircraft carriers led to heavy losses. To remedy the problem, the conversion of the liners *Roma* and *Augustus* into the aircraft carriers *Aquila* and *Sparviero*, which were never completed due to wartime events, was initiated.

Meanwhile, the Reggiane Re.2000 "Catapulable" fighter, employed on battleships, was introduced. After the armistice of September 8, 19 Ro.43 and 6 Re.2000 were operational. The carriers, almost completed, did not enter service: the *Aquila* was self-sunken to avoid capture.

▲ The catapult launch of an IMAM Ro. 43 from the stern of an Italian battleship. Small photo: a model of an IMAM Ro. 43 on the deck of a ship. Model made by Ezio Bottasini (courtesy).

IMAM (ROMEO) Ro. 43

IMAM Ro.43: THE SHIPBORNE RECONNAISSANCE SEAPLANE OF THE ITALIAN NAVY

Origin and development

In the 1930s, the Regia Marina initiated a program to equip its major ships with reconnaissance seaplanes. After experimenting with civilian models such as the Macchi M.18 and military models such as the Piaggio P.6 and CANT 25, a specification was issued in 1933 for a new aircraft with superior performance: speeds of 240 km/h and a range of 600 km or 5 hours and 30 minutes.

Several companies participated in the competition, including Piaggio, CMASA, CANT and IMAM (Industrie Meccaniche Aeronautiche Meridionali). The latter presented the Ro.43, designed by engineer Giovanni Galasso as a hydro version of the Ro.37 bis land biplane. The prototype, lighter and better performing than its competitors, flew for the first time on November 19, 1934, and exceeded expectations, winning the competition.

Production began in 1935 and continued until 1941, with more than 200 built, becoming the standard scout for major Italian naval units.

Technical characteristics and armament

The Ro.43 was a center-float biplane with a light but vulnerable to stress structure. The armament consisted of:

- 1 Breda-SAFAT 7.7-mm machine gun fixed in fighter (500 rounds).

- 1 rear brandishing machine gun, initially a Lewis, later replaced by another Breda-SAFAT (500 rounds). Optionally, a second forward machine gun could be installed.

Operational use and limitations

The Ro.43s were embarked on cruisers and battleships, including the *Littorio*, *Zara* and *Duca degli Abruzzi* classes, as well as the support ship *Giuseppe Miraglia*. However, structural problems quickly emerged:

▲ An IMAM Ro.43 embarked on a Littorio class battleship - Photo Ufficio Storico Marina Militare courtesy. Author's colouring. Small photo: an IMAM Ro.43 preserved in an Italian museum. Wiki cc1.

REGGIANE Re. 2000

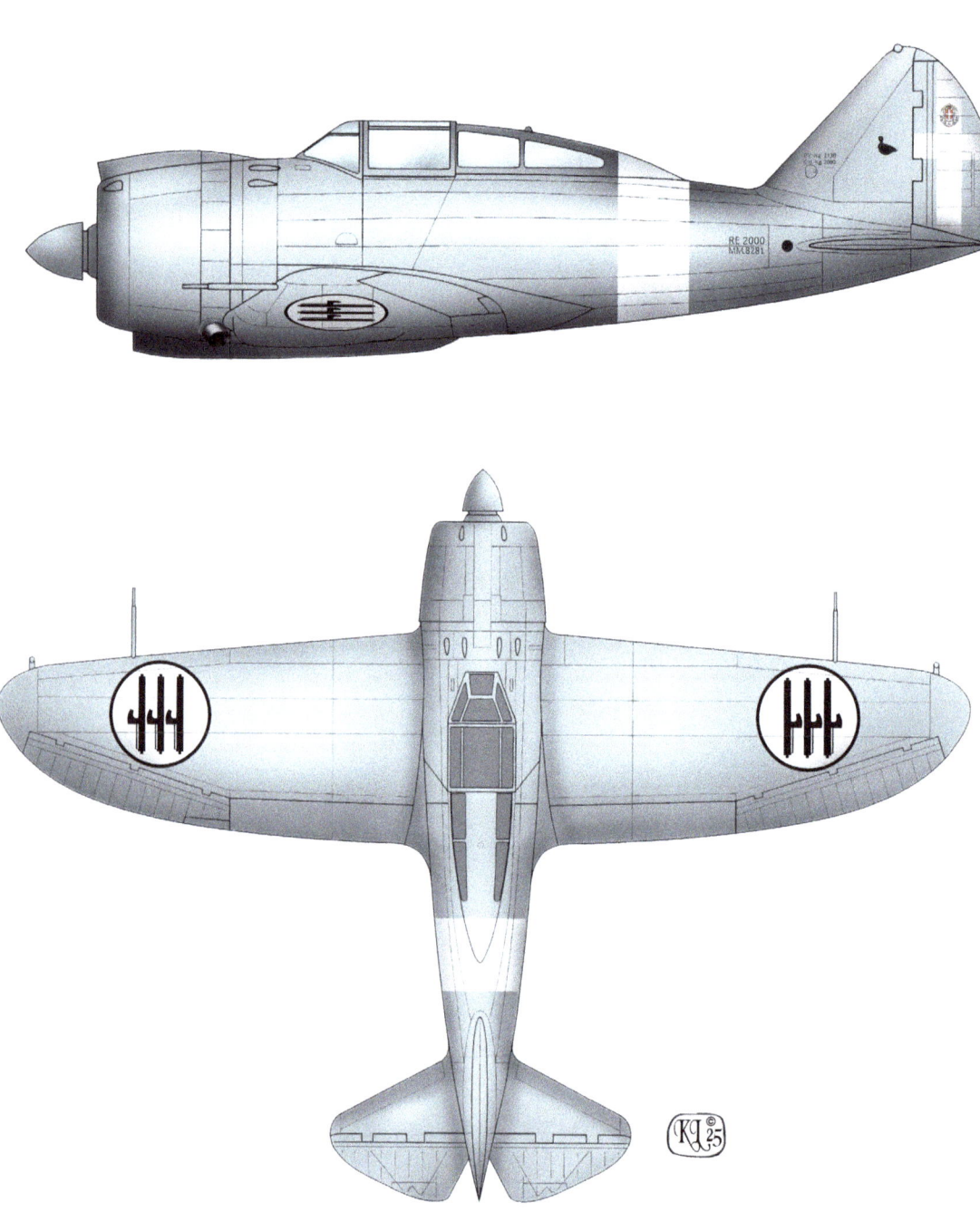

- Recovery operations with cranes often damaged the aircraft.
- Combat performance was inferior to that of opposing fighters, given the modest firepower.
- In rough sea conditions, re-boarding was nearly impossible, often forcing crews to reach the nearest seaport.

Despite these limitations, the lack of viable alternatives prolonged its use. During World War II, the Ro.43 was also employed as an improvised fighter, but unfortunately with poor results. After the disastrous Battle of Cape Matapan (1941), an attempt was made to replace it with the Reggiane Re.2000 Catapultabile, but the few available examples did not allow for a quick total replacement.

As of September 8, 1943, the date of the armistice, there were 19 Ro.43s still in service embarked and 20 assigned to Naval Forces Squadrons. Their careers ended as the airframes were depleted, supplanted by more modern aircraft or the abandonment of catapult seaplane operations. The aircraft acquired from Spain remained in operation until 1951.

Conclusions

The Ro.43 was an important aircraft for the Regia Marina, but its structural deficiencies and obsolescence limited its effectiveness. Although it was a step ahead of its predecessors, its history reflects the Italian naval aviation's difficulties in finding an effective solution for embarked reconnaissance during the conflict.

REGGIANE Re.2000: THE 'CATAPULT-LAUNCHABLE' FIGHTER OF THE ITALIAN NAVY

A project created for the Navy

In 1941, although the Reggiane Re.2000 had been excluded from the competition for the Regia Aeronautica's new fighter, the Regia Marina became interested in the aircraft because of its high range, superior to that of other Italian fighters. The idea was to employ it as a maritime reconnaissance and embarked fighter, launching it from the catapults of battleships.

Development and testing

In late 1941 and early 1942, two prototypes of the Reggiane Re. 2000 (MM.471 and MM.485) were modified to be launched from catapults. However, both were destroyed during testing: one in an accident in Taranto, the other during boarding operations. Therefore, a specimen already destined for Sweden

▲ A Reggiane Re. 2000 embarked on an Italian Navy unit, housed on the complicated catapult contraption, ready to be launched. Photo Ufficio Storico Marina Militare courtesy. Author's colouring.

(MM.8281) was requisitioned to continue the trials. Trials continued aboard the seaplane support ship *Giuseppe Miraglia*, where test pilot Lieutenant Giulio Reiner made the first successful takeoff on May 9, 1942. Despite initial successes, technical problems and the Navy's reluctance to risk the ships for further testing slowed the test program.

Operational use

Eventually, some Re.2000 "Catapultables" were finally assigned to the battleships *Vittorio Veneto, Littorio* (later renamed *Italia*) and *Roma*, as well as an Air Reserve Squadron of the Naval Forces. However, their use was very limited:

- Only operational mission: On August 23, 1943, a Re.2000 took off from *Vittorio Veneto* for an armed reconnaissance, later landing without any problems at Sarzana.

After the armistice (September 8, 1943):

 - *Roma* sank with her King.2000 still on board.

 - *Italy* (formerly *Littorio*) threw its plane into the sea after being hit.

 - Only the *Vittorio Veneto* managed to take off a Re.2000 against German aircraft, but the pilot was forced to land in Corsica, destroying the aircraft.

 - The last surviving King.2000 (MM.8287) reached Malta with the fleet and was then sent back to Italy.

Difficulties and limitations of the vehicle

- Technical problems: the Piaggio P.XI engine cooling system was unreliable, greatly limiting operation.

- Poor maneuverability: pilots, used to the Fiat C.R.42 biplanes, found it significantly less agile.

▲ Beautiful aerial shot of the IMAM Ro 43 water tanker with a two-man crew. Photo State Archives PD. In the small photo: the same vehicle mounted on the launching capstan of a ship.

- Poor combat results: despite a few missions, the only confirmed victory was against a downed Bristol Blenheim on June 24, 1942.

Several were the main versions of the craft, but we are interested in the one embarked on navy ships, i.e., the Series III ("Catapulable") craft-Adapted for launching from ships, with structural modifications and an enclosed rear canopy.

End of service

After the armistice, only 2-3 Re.2000s remained operational, used by the Cobelligerent Air Force without significant employment. The last remaining examples in northern Italy were either dismantled or requisitioned by the Luftwaffe. In conclusion, the Re.2000 Catapultabile was an innovative attempt, but hampered by many technical and organizational problems. Despite its potential, its use was marginal, demonstrating the Regia Marina's difficulties in integrating modern aircraft into naval operations.

▲ A Reggiane Re.2000 catapultable fighter just launched from the battleship *Vittorio Veneto*'s catapult. The aircraft is marked with a red "6" and lacks the sliding canopy. Wiki CC1 PD.

R.N.ROMA'S AIRCRAFT DATA SHEET		
Type	IMAM Ro.43	Reggiane Re. 2000
Seaplane Bases	Ind.Mec. Aer. Meridionali (IMAM)	Industrie Reggiane
Set - Launch - Completion	1934-1935-1951	1939 - 1945
Weight (in kg.)	1760-2400	2080-2839
Measures (in meters)	9,7 length- 11,50 wing - 3,5 height	7,99 length - 11 wing - 3,2 height
Engine	Piaggio P.X R radial	Piaggio P.XI RC.40 radial
Maximum speed	315 km/h	530 km/h
Autonomy	800/1500 km	740 km
Crew	1/2	1
Armament	2 Breda-SAFAT 7.7 mm calibre	2 Breda-SAFAT 12.7 mm
Users	Italy - Spain	Italy - Hungary - Sweden
Total production	217	158

▲ Launch of the *Vittorio Veneto*, Trieste, 25 July 1937.

▼ The *Littorio*, in the foreground, and the *Vittorio Veneto* during an exercise in the waters off Taranto, in the summer of 1940.

THE OTHER SHIPS OF THE LITTORIO CLASS

■ THE BATTLESHIP VITTORIO VENETO: A GIANT OF THE ROYAL NAVY

The *Vittorio Veneto* was one of the most powerful battleships of the Italian Royal Navy during World War II, belonging to the *Littorio* class (sometimes also called the *Vittorio Veneto* class). Considered the flagship of Italy's wartime naval shipbuilding industry, she represented a technological leap from previous units due to her advanced features and firepower.

Design and construction

The design of the *Vittorio Veneto* was entrusted to General Umberto Pugliese and Engineer Francesco Mazzullo, who developed a battleship capable of overcoming the limitations imposed by the Washington Naval Treaty (1922), which set the maximum displacement for battleships at 35,000 tons. The *Vittorio Veneto*, however, achieved a higher displacement, demonstrating Italian ambition to compete with the most powerful navies of the time.

Construction began on October 28, 1934, at Shipyards Riuniti dell'Adriatico (CRDA) in Trieste, the same shipyard that would later launch her sister ship, *Roma*. After launching on July 25, 1937, the ship was completed on April 28, 1940, equipped with IMAM Ro.43 reconnaissance seaplanes. She officially entered service on August 2, 1940, shortly after Italy entered the world conflict, and was assigned to the IX Armored Division of the I Naval Squadron, based in Taranto.

Wartime operations in the Mediterranean

During the war, the *Vittorio Veneto* participated in 56 missions, 11 of which were dedicated to hunting enemy ships. Her first significant action occurred on August 31, 1940, when, together with the *Littorio* and other fleet units, she attempted to intercept the British Fleet engaged in Operation Hats. However, due to adverse weather conditions and failure to detect the enemy, the mission ended without a confrontation. On the night of November 11-12, 1940, during the British raid on Taranto (known as "Taranto Night"), the *Vittorio Veneto* was attacked by torpedo bombers, but a torpedo prematurely exploded without hitting her. On September 29, however, she took part in Operation MB 5, an action to counter Allied convoys. The first real test of fire came during the Battle of Cape Teulada (Nov. 27, 1940), where the battleship, under the command of Captain Giuseppe Sparzani and with Admiral Inigo Campioni on board as commander of the 1ªSquadron Naval, engaged in an intense clash with British cruisers. The *Vittorio Veneto* fired 19 381 mm rounds from the aft tower, forcing the enemy formation to retreat.

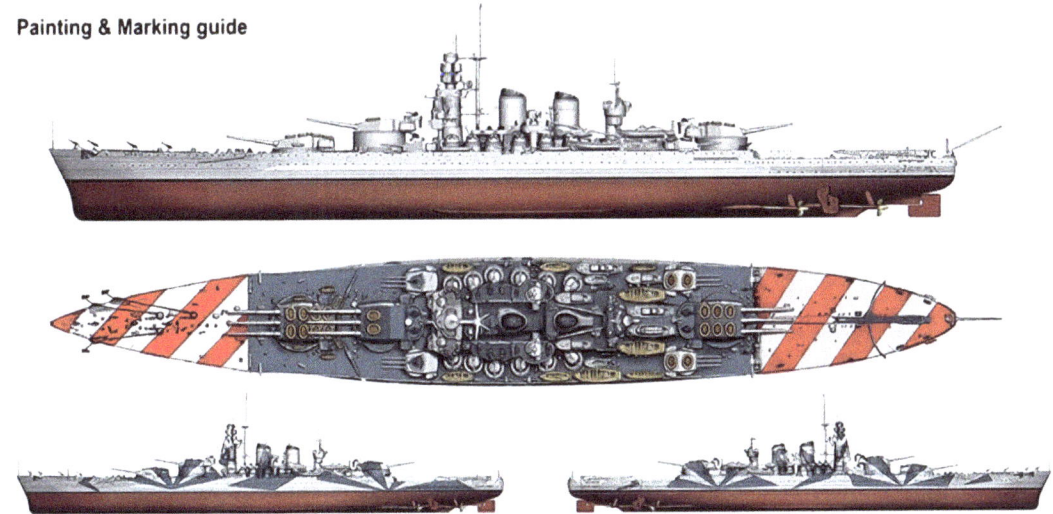

▲ Profiles of the *Vittorio Veneto* taken from the Trumpeter (China models) courtesy modelling kit.

Damage and repairs

On January 8, 1941, while in Naples, the ship suffered a British air attack without damage, but as a precaution she was transferred to La Spezia. A few days later, on March 26, 1941, she sailed as Admiral Angelo Iachino's flagship for what was to become the Battle of Cape Matapan. During the Battle of Gaudo (March 28), the *Vittorio Veneto* attempted to encircle the British cruisers, but her shots missed their targets. Shortly thereafter, at 3:20 p.m., she was hit by a torpedo bomber near her port propeller, taking on 4,000 tons of water and temporarily losing power. Despite the damage, she managed to resume sailing at 16-19 knots, but an attempt to rescue the cruiser *Pola* (immobilized by another torpedo) led to the disaster at Cape Matapan, with the loss of two cruisers and two Italian destroyers.

After four months of repairs, the ship returned to service in July 1941, participating in other missions, including an attempt to intercept the British convoy "Halberd" (Sept. 27, 1941).

On December 14, 1941, during a transfer from Naples to Taranto, she was torpedoed by the British submarine HMS *Urge*, sustaining severe damage but managing to reach port thanks to the Pugliese absorber cylinders, which limited the effects of the explosion. Repairs lasted until the spring of 1942.

The last action and operational decline

In 1942, the *Vittorio Veneto* was the first Italian battleship to be equipped with an E.C. 4 "Owl" radar, greatly improving night detection capabilities.

Her last significant action was during the Battle of Mid-June (June 14-16, 1942), when, together with the *Littorio*, she attempted to intercept the British "Vigorous" convoy. Although there were no direct clashes, the threat posed by the two Italian battleships forced the British to retreat.

After this mission, fuel shortages and the risk of air and underwater attacks drastically limited the operations of the large Italian battleships.

R.N. VITTORIO VENETO DATA SHEET	
Type	**Battleship - Littorio Class**
Shipyards	C.R.D.A San Marco Trieste
Setup -Launch- In service	October 1934 / July 1937/ August 1940/ Destroyed in 1948
Displacement	43.624 t - 45.752 t full loaded
Measures (in meters)	Length: 238. Width: 33, Draught: 10,5
Propulsion	8 boilers, 4 Belluzzo turbines, 4 propellers Power: 130/140,000 hp
Maximum speed	30 knots (56 km/h)
Autonomy	3920 miles at 20 knots (with 4000 t of naphtha)
Crew	1830 (1910 as flagship)
Onboard sensors	Radar EC3/bis
Gun armament	-9 × 381/50 Model 1934 (three triple turrets) -12 × 152/55 mm Model 1936 (four triple turrets) -12 × 90/50 mm AA Model 1939 (twelve single turrets)
Deck machine guns	-20 × 37/54 mm AA Breda Model 1932 (8 twin mounts + 4 single mounts) -32 × 20/65 mm AA Model 1935 (16 twin mounts)
Armour	350 mm (vertical) 150/207 mm (horizontal above ammunition magazines) 350 mm (max. main artillery) 280 mm (max. secondary artillery) 260 mm (command tower)
Aircrafts	3 between IMAM Ro.43 and Reggiane Re.2000

The Armistice and the end

After the Armistice of September 8, 1943, the *Vittorio Veneto* was among the units that reached Malta to surrender to the Allies. It was during the same transfer that the sister ship *Roma* was sunk by a German radio-guided bomb, the first use of such a weapon in history.

The *Vittorio Veneto* and *Littorio* (renamed *Italia*) were then interned in the Amari Lakes (Egypt). Despite some proposals to employ them alongside the Allies, Peace Treaty clauses mandated their demolition, which took place starting in 1948.

THE BATTLESHIP LITTORIO: THE FLAGSHIP OF THE ROYAL NAVY

The *Littorio*, renamed *Italia* on July 30, 1943, was the first and most representative battleship of its class, which also included the *Vittorio Veneto* and *Roma*. Designed to be the flagship of the Italian fleet during World War II, she represented the highest technological and industrial effort of the Royal Navy. Despite her excellent technical characteristics, her operational use was limited by the prudence of naval commands and, after 1942, her wartime activity was drastically reduced.

Construction and commissioning

The *Littorio* was laid down at Ansaldo Shipyards in Genoa on October 28, 1934, launched on August 22, 1937, and entered service on May 6, 1940, shortly before Italy's entry into the war. However, she was not yet fully operational at the outbreak of hostilities.

Assigned to the IX Armored Division of the I Naval Squadron, she became Admiral Carlo Bergamini's flagship. She was equipped with three IMAM Ro.43 seaplanes for reconnaissance and had powerful armament: nine 381 mm, 12 152 mm, 12 90 mm anti-aircraft guns and an underwater protection system designed by General Umberto Pugliese.

R.N. LITTORIO (THEN ITALIA FROM 30 JULY 1943) DATA SHEET	
Type	Battleship - Littorio Class
Shipyards	Ansaldo Genova
Setup -Launch- In service	October 1934 / August 1937/ May 1940/ Destroyed in 1948
Displacement	43.835 t - 45.963 t full loaded
Measures (in meters)	Length: 238. Width: 33, Draught: 10,5
Propulsion	8 boilers, 4 Belluzzo turbines, 4 propellers Power: 130/140,000 hp
Maximum speed	30 knots (56 km/h)
Autonomy	3920 miles at 20 knots (with 4000 t of naphtha)
Crew	120 officers and 1,800 non-commissioned officers and municipalities
Onboard sensors	Radar EC3/bis installato solo nel 1942.
Gun armament	-9 × 381/50 Model 1934 (three triple turrets) -12 × 152/55 mm Model 1936 (four triple turrets) -12 × 90/50 mm AA Model 1939 (twelve single turrets)
Deck machine guns	-20 × 37/54 mm AA Breda Model 1932 (8 twin mounts + 4 single mounts) -28 × 20/65 mm AA Model 1935 (14 twin mounts)
Armour	350 mm (vertical) 150/207 mm (horizontal above ammunition magazines) 350 mm (max. main artillery) 280 mm (max. secondary artillery) 260 mm (command tower)
Aircrafts	3 between IMAM Ro.43 and Reggiane Re.2000

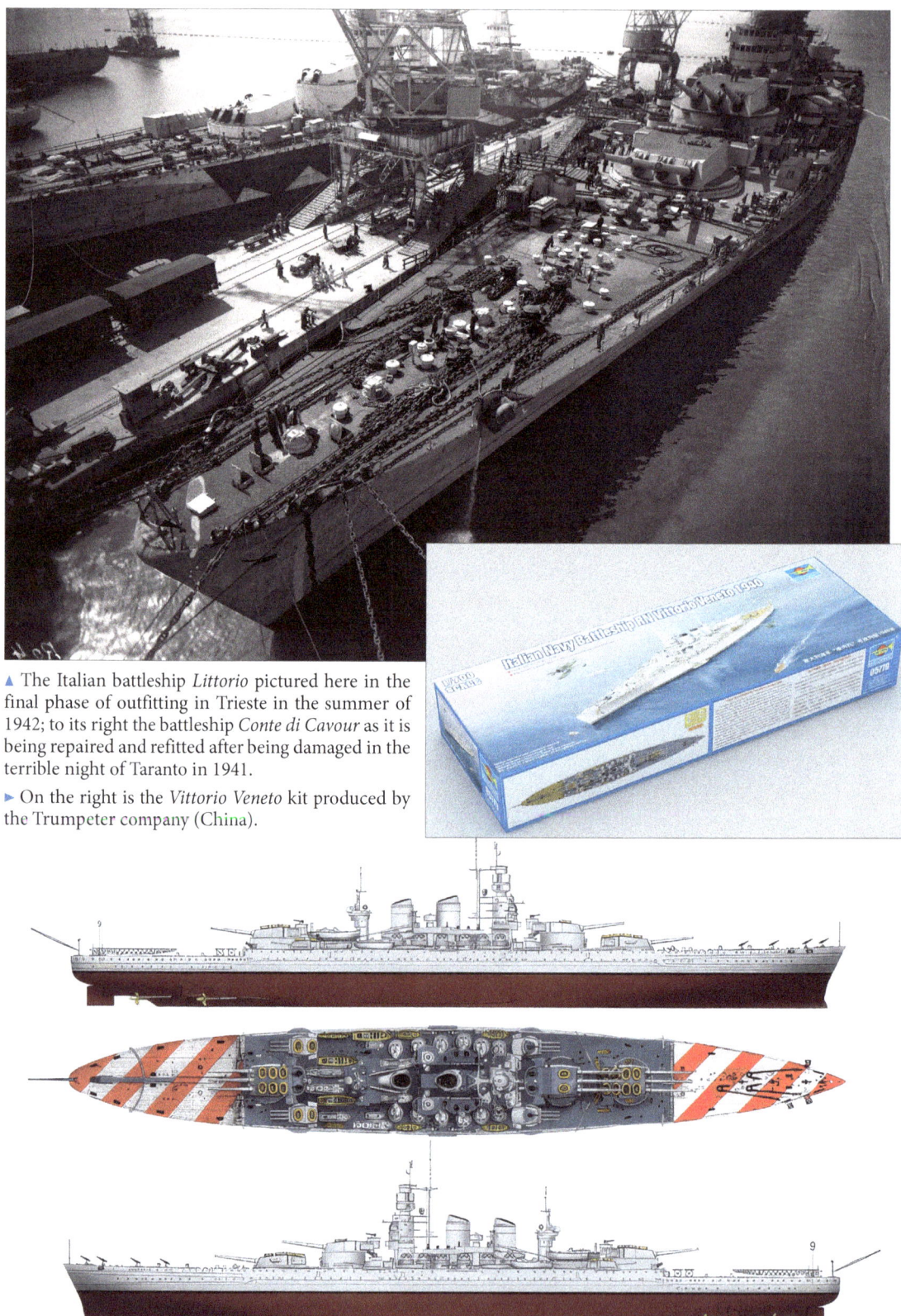

▲ The Italian battleship *Littorio* pictured here in the final phase of outfitting in Trieste in the summer of 1942; to its right the battleship *Conte di Cavour* as it is being repaired and refitted after being damaged in the terrible night of Taranto in 1941.

▶ On the right is the *Vittorio Veneto* kit produced by the Trumpeter company (China).

▲ *Littorio* profiles from the Trumpeter (China models) courtesy model kit.

▲ The Italian battleship *Vittorio Veneto* photographed in roadstead in 1940 before its completion. Note the lack of rangefinders.

War operations

The Taranto Attack (Nov. 11-12, 1940) - During the British raid on Taranto, the *Littorio* was hit by three torpedoes fired by Fairey Swordfish torpedo bombers. One of the torpedoes caused severe flooding, but thanks to Pugliese absorber cylinders, the ship avoided irreparable damage. After six months of repairs, she returned to service, surprising the British who thought they had put her out of commission for good.

The Second Battle of Sirte (March 22, 1942) - Under the command of Admiral Angelo Iachino, the *Littorio* engaged a British naval formation. Its 381 mm guns severely damaged the destroyer HMS *Kingston* and HMS *Havock*, while a 152 mm shell hit the cruiser HMS *Cleopatra*. However, the battle ended without decisive results due to the Italian command's lack of aggressiveness.

The Battle of Mid-June (June 14-16, 1942) - Together with the *Vittorio Veneto*, the *Littorio* attempted to intercept the British convoy "Vigorous" bound for Malta. During the operation, she was hit in the bow by a torpedo launched from a British plane and grazed by a U.S. bomb, but managed to return to port without serious consequences.

The Bombardment of La Spezia (1943) - April 18-19, 1943: An aerial bombardment slightly damaged the *Littorio* and sank the destroyer *Alpino*.

- June 5, 1943: A new air attack damaged the *Roma* and *Vittorio Veneto*, leaving the *Littorio* as the only operational battleship until the other two were repaired.

The name change: from *Littorio* to *Italia*

After the fall of Fascism (July 25, 1943), the Badoglio government renamed the ship "*Italia*" (July 30) to remove any reference to the regime. Until the armistice on September 8, the ship had completed 46 missions, including nine to search for the enemy and three to escort domestic traffic.

On Sept. 9, 1943, the Italian fleet sailed from La Spezia to Malta, as stipulated in the armistice agreements. However, instead of raising the black plumes (a sign of surrender), the *Roma*, flagship, displayed the grand pavese, a symbolic gesture of pride. During the subsequent German attack carried by 28 Luft-

▲ The Italian battleship *Littorio* at sea before the war. Wiki CC1 PD.

waffe Dornier Do 217 bombers that attacked the fleet with Fritz X radio-guided bombs, *Italy* suffered the following damage:

- A first bomb fell near the Italia, temporarily blocking its rudder. The R.N. *Italia,* though damaged, managed to continue toward Malta, escorted by the destroyers *Mitragliere and Carabiniere.*

Internment and demolition

After arriving in Malta, the Allies briefly considered deploying *the Italia* and *Vittorio Veneto* to the Pacific, but discarded the idea due to technical and political problems. The two ships were then interned in the Amari Lakes (Egypt) until 1947. Despite Italian attempts to preserve them, the Peace Treaty mandated their scrapping:

- The U.S. gave up taking it over.
- The USSR demanded the dismantling of the main guns.
- Between 1948 and 1955, the Italia (formerly *Littorio*) and *Vittorio Veneto* were decommissioned and scrapped, marking the end of an era for the Italian Navy.

■ THE BATTLESHIP IMPERO: THE SHIP NEVER FINISHED

The *Impero* was a battleship belonging to the Regia Marina, designed as the third unit of the *Littorio* class. The unit was launched on November 15, 1939, close to the start of World War II. According to the Navy's initial plans, the ship was to be completed by December 1941, in time to be operational during the crucial phases of the war. However, changing strategic and production needs forced an abrupt halt to the program.

The wartime priority quickly shifted to upgrading light naval vessels-such as destroyers, torpedo boats, and anti-submarine units-leaving the construction of large battleships on the back burner. Although the outfitting of the *Impero* was transferred to Trieste for completion, it proceeded uneventfully until it was finally suspended in July 1943, with the hull reaching about 77 percent of completion. Subsequently captured by German forces after the armistice of September 8, 1943, the ship was later sunk in port by American aerial bombardment. Salvaged after the war, her hull was scrapped in the late 1940s.

Construction and transfers

Also designed by naval engineer Umberto Pugliese, the *Impero* was laid down on May 14, 1938 at the Sestri Ponente Shipyard in Genoa. The launching took place a year and a half later, on November 15, 1939. With Italy nearing entry into the war (June 1940), the hull was towed from Genoa, considered too exposed to French and British air attacks, to the port of Brindisi, where it arrived on June 8, 1940, two days before the official declaration of war.

The transfer of equipment needed to complete the unit to Trieste was suspended, however, as the Regia Marina's production priorities focused on upgrading light and anti-submarine units. Thus, materials intended for the *Impero* - laminates, sections, plant - were diverted to other shipyards and other programs. The *Impero* thus remained stationary in Brindisi throughout 1941.

In January 1942, it was decided to continue outfitting work: the ship, employing part of its own engine apparatus, was transferred to Venice on January 22 and later, in November of that year, reached the Shipyards Riuniti dell'Adriatico (CRDA) in Trieste. However, the worsening war situation and the shortage of materials prevented any further progress. At the same time, an attempt to restore the battleship Conte di Cavour, badly damaged in Taranto, also proved futile. When the armistice was announced on September 8, 1943, the *Impero*'s incomplete hull was abandoned, deemed to be of no operational use. German forces, which occupied Trieste in the following days, took possession of the unit. In June 1944, the German naval command decided to employ some captured Italian ships to conduct tests of structural resistance to explosives. After unsuccessfully examining the hulls of the cruisers *Bolzano* and *Gorizia* in La Spezia, the technicians went to Trieste, where the hull of the *Impero* was found to be suitable for such tests, in part due to the presence of the underwater torpedo protection system known as the "Pugliese cylinders."

At the time of inspection, the battleship was in an advanced but incomplete state: The main armored deck was largely completed and welded, but openings remained for work in progress. The armored doors and superstructures were missing. The 381 mm towers I and II had no guns or cradles, while tower III was not yet mounted as it was still on the ground. The engine apparatus was partially completed, with the forward boilers finished and the aft boilers at 40 percent. The ship was manned by sixty workers from the Ansaldo company, and was in very good overall condition.

Then on Feb. 20, 1945, a heavy aerial bombardment conducted by the United States Army Air Forces hit the port of Trieste: the *Impero* was severely damaged by the explosions and lay on the seabed due to extensive flooding. Already on February 15 a similar fate had befallen the Conte di Cavour, which never recovered after Taranto. In early 1949 the wreck was finally taken to Porto Marghera, where final dismantling took place.

▲ The Italian battleship *Vittorio Veneto* photographed from a low-flying aircraft as it prepares to take to the sea on its way out of Taranto harbour. Central State Archive PD.

▲ The Italian Littorio Class battleships at sea.

LA BATTLESHIP ROMA: THE MODELS

The model production of the R.N. *Roma* and its sisters *Vittorio Veneto* and *Littorio* is very widespread. Several are the modeling houses that try their hand at the means of our Navy, in addition to Italeri, we recall Trumpeter (China), Tamiya (Japan), Revell and many others. Italian authors also do their best in self-builds in every scale of our battleships and cruisers. Especially in the 1:350 or 1:700 scale. In this review, the good Roman model maker Matteo d'Aniello takes the lead with a successful, award-winning model of the Battleship *Roma* in 1:350 scale. Also very interesting are models by other modelers but especially by the doyen of Italian modeling, ace Maurizio Maggi!

Others are elaborations of various authors and modelers photographed by the author of the book in various competitions. Where it has been possible we dutifully quote the authors' names.

■ THE R.N. BATTLESHIP ROMA BY MATTEO D'ANIELLO

Below is a series of images of the *Roma* ship executed by D'Aniello, captions are by the author. Matteo D'Aniello was born in Rome in 1987. Passionate about history and military modeling since childhood, over the years he found his greatest inspiration in naval subjects. Thanks to the quality and accuracy of his models, he quickly established himself in the Italian naval modeling scene.

▲ Image depicting the midship superstructure from the starboard side. The model was built starting from the Trumpeter 1:350 scale kit and was enhanced with small scratch-built details, resin parts, and dedicated photo-etch sets.

WW2 ITALIAN NAVY COLORS & CAMOUFLAGE

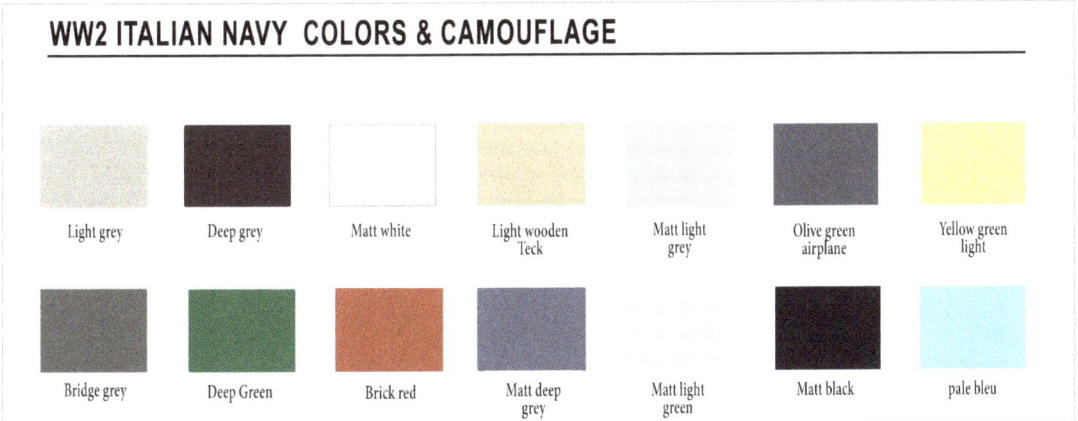

The two images show a full view of the starboard side and an overhead view, respectively. Note the darker shade of the deck and walkable surfaces compared to the hull sides and vertical surfaces for camouflage purposes. The aft deck, however, is covered in natural teak, a feature reserved only for the most prestigious naval units.

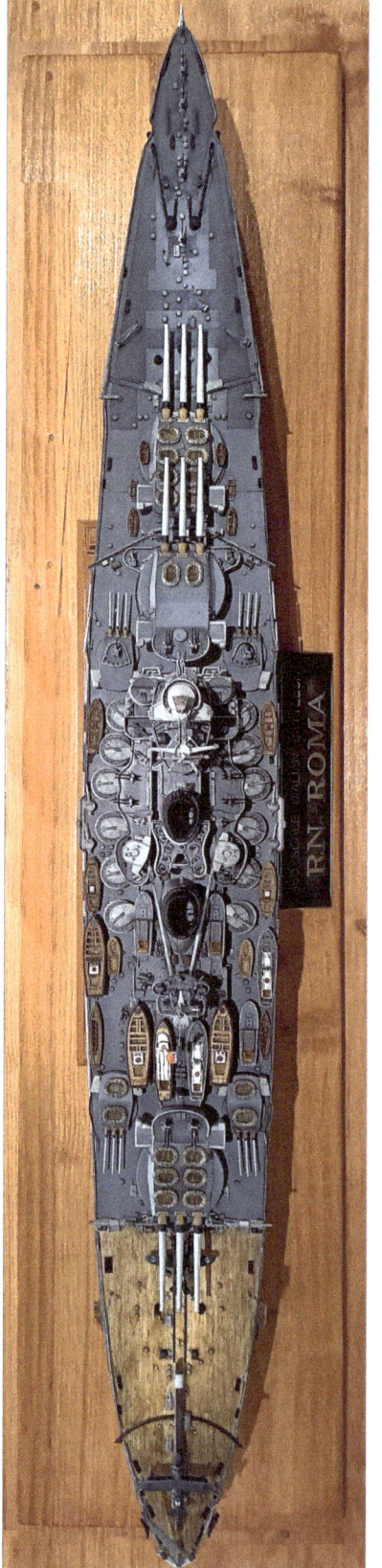

View of the starboard garden (officer's terrace). In the foreground, the ship's name in brass is preceded by the fascio littorio (a fascist symbol). Visible are the large main rudder, the auxiliary starboard rudder; and the propellers with their shafts and supports. The thickening from the armored belt along the hull near the waterline is clearly seen, followed by the bulge of the Pugliese torpedo defense system. The aft portholes belong to the officers' quarters.

First image: The ship seen from the port bow. Second image: A close-up of the starboard side, clearly showing the boarding ladder used for sea stops. The large armored turret of the aft triple 381/50mm main battery and the armored turret of the triple 152/55 mm secondary battery are visible.

(First photo) View of the battleship Roma's port side, highlighting its extremely harmonious lines, the result of meticulous design. (Second photo) In the foreground, the 152mm armored turret with a barbette housing the twin 20/65mm Breda AA gun on top. Above it is the massive 381/50mm turret positioned ahead of the forecastle. Note the raised platform holding another twin 20/65mm Breda AA mount on the main turret. Also visible is the paravane (mine-clearing device) placed between the two main turrets. (Third photo) Image showing the arrangement of the forward main guns. On the lower left of the forecastle deck is the crane used for transporting and deploying the paravane, with its boom folded against the hull.

BATTLESHIP ROMA WWII

(First image) View of the teak-covered aft deck, housing the oscillating catapult system for the two Ro.43 and Reggiane 2000 aircraft, along with the recovery crane for the seaplane.

(Second image) Close-up of the aft superstructure, featuring 105cm and 150cm searchlights, the maneuvering signal mast (circle and diamond), the flag mast, and a 3M fire control director for AA artillery. Visible is the telescopic boom crane for handling light boats, operated by its winch on the deckhouse.

The images show the radio reception antenna system (called aereo) with its rigging, the lookout station between the two funnels, and the AA gun positions occupied by twin 20/65mm (short-range) and 37/54mm (medium-range) guns, along with spotting binoculars and the 5M fire control director for the 152/55m guns. Further down on the main deck are the six 90/53mm AA guns for long-range barrage fire (and anti-small craft when needed). Below them are the two 120/40mm illuminating howitzers.

BATTLESHIP ROMA WWII

(First image) Side view of the forward large-caliber turret. (Second image) The admiral's 10-meter motorboat placed on the deckhouse, with the 12.25m diesel boat on the main deck.

(Third image) View of the command tower housing the EC3/ter Gufo radar, followed by the two large adjustable rangefinders for the BGS main battery fire control. Below is the secondary conning tower, then the main bridge flanked by 3M AA fire control directors and lookout posts.

(Fourth image) Close-up of the forward trinates 381/50mm turret with its AA mount consisting of two twins Breda 37/54mm guns, flanked by two 152/55mm turrets equipped with barbettes for twin 20/65mm Breda guns.

(Fifth image) Framing of the starboard side with the boat cranes. The mainmast is partially visible, with the flag locker at its base where the radio signal rigging (from the aereo) connects. Above is the crow's nest, signal halyards, and supporting rigging for the yards.

THE ROMA IN 3D

The battleship *Roma* PD made in 3D by "Cbhierro" who released it in PD with the following text: *I, the copyright holder of this work, release this work into the public domain. This applies worldwide. In some countries this may not be legally possible; if so: I grant anyone the right to use this work for any purpose, without any conditions, unless such conditions are required by law. RM*

68 | TWE

BATTLESHIP ROMA WWII

BATTLESHIP ROMA WWII

BIBLIOGRAPHY

-Franco Bargoni, Franco Gay, Orizzonte Mare - *Corazzate classe Vittorio Veneto, parte I*, Roma, Bizzarri, 1973.

-Franco Bargoni, Franco Gay, Orizzonte Mare - *Corazzate classe Vittorio Veneto, parte II*, Roma, Bizzarri, 1973.

-P. Ramoino, *La "minaccia" navale francese negli anni venti e trenta del xx secolo*, su marina.difesa.it. URL consultato l'8 settembre 2011.

-John Campbell, *Naval Weapons of World War II*, Annapolis, Naval Institute Press, 1985.

-William H Garzke, Battleships: *Axis and Neutral Battleships in World War II*, Annapolis, Naval Institute Press, 1995, ISBN 0-87021-101-3.

-John Roberts, *Italy in Conway's All the World's Fighting Ships 1922–1946*, Greenwich, Conway Maritime Press, 1980, ISBN 0851771467.

-Mark Stille, *Italian Battleships of World War II*, Oxford, Osprey Publishing, 2011.

-Gianni Rocca, *Fucilate gli ammiragli. La tragedia della Marina italiana nella seconda guerra mondiale,* Mondadori, 1987, ISBN 978-88-04-43392-7.

-Augusto de Toro, *Dalle "Littorio" alle "Impero". Navi da battaglia, studi e programmi navali in Italia nella seconda metà degli anni Trenta*, in Bollettino d'Archivio dell'Ufficio Storico della Marina Militare, Roma, Ufficio Storico della Marina Militare, marzo 2012, pp. 1-47.

-Paolo Alberini e Franco Prosperini, *Uomini della marina 1861-1946 dizionario biografico,* Roma, Ufficio Storico della Marina Militare, 2016, ISBN 978-88-98485-95-6.

-Erminio Bagnasco, Augusto De Toro, Le navi da battaglia, classe *Littorio* (1937-1948), 2ª ed., Albertelli, 2010, ISBN 88-87372-66-7.

-Marc'Antonio Bragadin, *La Marina italiana 1940-1945*, Odoya, 2011, ISBN 978-88-6288-110-4.

-Robert Gardiner e Roger Chesneau, *All the World Fighting's Ships 1922-1946*, Annapolis, MD, Naval Institute Press, 1980, ISBN 978-0-85177-146-5.

-Giorgio Giorgerini, Ermanno Martino, Riccardo Nassigh, *Storia della Marina, a cura di Giorgio Giorgerini, volume III*, Milano, Fabbri, 1978.

-Francesco Mattesini, *8 settembre 1943 la Regia marina nella tragedia dell'Italia vol. 1 e 2* , Soldiershop- Luca Cristini editore Bergamo 2020.

-Arrigo Petacco, *La flotta si arrende, in La nostra guerra 1940-1945. L'avventura bellica tra bugie e verità,* Milano, A. Mondadori, 1996, ISBN 88-04-41325-5.

-Marco Santarini, *La condotta del tiro navale da bordo nella Regia Marina 1900-1945,* Roma, Ufficio storico della marina militare, 2017, ISBN 9788899642105.

-Domenico Carro, Gennaro Baretta, *Corazzata Roma*, Cooperativa Eureka Roma 2011

- A.Perepeczko, *Wtoskie pancerniki typu Vittorio Veneto*, Magnum X Varsavia 2005

-Maurizio Brescia, *Mussolini's Navy* Seaforth Publishing 2012, ISBN 978 1 84832 115 1

-Ugo Gerini, *Corazzata Roma. Destinazione finale. Dal golfo di Trieste a quello dell'Asinara.* Luglio editore, Trieste 2015

-Ugo Gerini, Corazzata Roma. *Una storia per immagini. Ediz. illustrata* Luglio editore, Trieste 2017

PUBLISHED TITLES

TWE-040 EN

www.ingramcontent.com/pod-product-compliance
Ingram Content Group UK Ltd.
Pitfield, Milton Keynes, MK11 3LW, UK
UKHW060216240426
12048UKWH00030BB/1691